WOMEN POETS OF JAPAN

BOOKS BY KENNETH REXROTH

POEMS

The Collected Shorter Poems
The Collected Longer Poems
Sky Sea Birds Trees Earth House Beasts Flowers
New Poems
The Morning Star
Selected Poems

PLAYS

Beyond the Mountains

CRITICISM & ESSAYS

The Alternative Society
American Poetry in the Twentieth Century
Assays
Bird in the Bush
The Classics Revisited
Communalism, from the Neolithic to 1900
The Elastic Retort
With Eye and Ear

TRANSLATIONS

100 Poems from the Chinese
100 More Poems from the Chinese:
  Love and the Turning Year
Seasons of Sacred Lust: The
  Selected Poems of Kazuko Shiraishi
  (with Ikiko Atsumi, John Solt, Carol Tinker,
  and Yasuyo Morita)
Women Poets of Japan
  (with Ikiko Atsumi)
Woman Poets of China
  (with Ling Chung)
100 French Poems
Poems from the Greek Anthology
100 Poems from the Japanese
100 More Poems from the Japanese
30 Spanish Poems of Love and Exile
Selected Poems of Pierre Reverdy
Li Ch'ing-chao: Complete Poems
  (with Ling Chung)

AUTOBIOGRAPHY

An Autobiographical Novel

EDITOR

An Anthology of Pre-literate Poetry
The Continuum Poetry Series

WOMEN POETS
OF
JAPAN

Translated and Edited by

KENNETH REXROTH
AND IKUKO ATSUMI

A NEW DIRECTIONS BOOK

Formerly published by The Seabury Press as *The Burning Heart*.
First published as New Directions Paperbook 527 in 1982. Pub-
lished simultaneously in Canada by Penguin Books Canada
Limited.

Library of Congress Cataloging in Publication Data

Burning heart.
    Women poets of Japan.
    (A New Directions Book)
    Previously published as: The Burning heart.
1977.
    "New Directions paperback 527."
    1. Japanese poetry—Translations into English.
2. English poetry—Translations from Japanese.
3. Japanese poetry—Women authors—History and
criticism.   I. Rexroth, Kenneth, 1905–
II. Atsumi, Ikuko.   III. Title.
PL782.E3B84   1982   895.6′1′00809287   81-18693
ISBN 0-8112-0820-6 (pbk.)   AACR2

New Directions Books are published for James Laughlin
by New Directions Publishing Corporation,
80 Eighth Avenue, New York 10011

FOURTH PRINTING

CONTENTS

Authors' Note   ix

CLASSIC POETS
Princess Nukada (7th Century)   3
Empress Jitō (645–702)   6
Ōtomo no Sakanoe no Iratsume (8th Century)   8
Yosami, Wife of Hitomaro (8th Century)   10
Lady Kii (8th Century)   12
Kasa no Iratsume (8th Century)   13
Ono no Komachi (9th Century)   14
Lady Ise (9-10th Century)   17
Shirome (10th Century)   19
Lady Ukon (10th Century)   20
Murasaki Shikibu (974-1031)   21
Akazome Emon (?–1027)   23
Sei Shōnagon (10th Century)   25
Mother of Michitsuna (10th Century)   26
Daini no Sanmi (10-11th Century)   27
Izumi Shikibu (11th Century)   28
Ise Tayū (11th Century)   30
Lady Sagami (11th Century)   34
Lady Suwo (11-12th Century)   35
Princess Shikishi (?–1201)   36
Kenrei Mon-in Ukyō no Daibu (12th Century)   37
Giō (12th Century)   38
Yokobue (12th Century)   39
Shizuka (12th Century)   40
Lady Horikawa (12th Century)   41
The Daughter of Minamoto no Toshitaka
  (12th Century)   42
Shunzei's Daughter (1171?–1252?)   43

Abutsu-Ni (1209–1283)   45

HAIKU POETS OF THE TOKUGAWA PERIOD
Kawai Chigetsu-Ni (1632–1736)   49
Den Sute-Jo (1633–1698)   50
Ōme Shushiki (1668–1725)   51
Chine-Jo (Late 17th Century)   52
Fukuda Chiyo-Ni (1703–1775)   53
Ukihashi (Late 17th Century)   55
Enomoto Seifu-Jo (1731–1814)   56
Matsumoto Koyū-Ni (Late 18th Century)   57
Imaizumi Sogetsu-Ni (?–1804)   58
Tagami Kikusha-Ni (1752–1826)   59

MODERN TANKA POETS
Yosano Akiko (1878–1942)   63
Yamakawa Tomiko (1879–1909)   67
Chino Masako (1880–1946)   68
Kujō Takeko (1887–1928)   69
Okamoto Kanoko (1889–1939)   70
Gotō Miyoko (1898–   )   71
Hatsui Shizue (1900–   )   72
Anryū Suharu (1923–   )   73
Baba Akiko (1928–   )   74

MODERN HAIKU POETS
Sugita Hisajo (1890–1946)   79
Mitsuhashi Takajo (1899–1972)   80
Hashimoto Takako (1899–1963)   81
Nakamura Teijo (1900–   )   82
Hoshino Tatsuko (1903–   )   83
Yagi Mikajo (1924–   )   84

FREE VERSE POETS

Yosano Akiko (1878–1942)   87
Fukao Sumako (1893–1974)   88
Hayashi Fumiko (1904–1951)   89
Nagase Kiyoko (1906–   )   90
Nakamura Chio (1913–   )   91
Takada Toshiko (1916–   )   92
Takiguchi Masako (1918–   )   93
Mitsui Futabako (1919–   )   95
Ishigaki Rin (1920–   )   96
Shindō Chie (1920–   )   99
Ibaragi Noriko (1926–   )   100
Fukunaka Tomoko (1928–   )   102
Fukui Hisako (1929–   )   104
Shinkawa Kazue (1929–   )   105
Inoue Michiko (?–   )   106
Tada Chimako (1930–   )   107
Shiraishi Kazuko (1931–   )   108
Yoshihara Sachiko (1932–   )   118
Kōra Rumiko (1932–   )   123
Tomioka Taeko (1935–   )   124
Yoshiyuki Rie (1939–   )   126
Atsumi Ikuko (1940–   )   127
Kanai Mieko (1947–   )   129
Nishi Junko (?–   )   132

ANONYMOUS GEISHA SONGS   135

I. Notes on the Poets   140
II. The Women Poets of Japan—A Brief Survey   161
III. Table of Japanese Historical Periods   183

AUTHORS' NOTE

KENNETH REXROTH and Ikuko Atsumi are the initial and final translators but we both have been aided by John Solt, Carol Tinker, and Morita Yasuyo. Many of the classical poems are the work of Rexroth alone or with the advice of Morito Yasuyo. The typescript was read over in its first draft by Professor Kodama Sanehide of Doshisha Women's College who offered valuable advice. Many of the poems have been published in a wide variety of American literary magazines and the translators wish to acknowledge their gratitude to the editors who usually welcomed them with enthusiasm.

The calligraphy—the name of each poet—is by Machi Shunsō, usually considered the greatest woman calligrapher in Japan. She has exhibited her work all over the world and is in many public and private collections, both in the West and in Japan.

Kenneth Rexroth would like to dedicate the book to Morita Yasuyo and Carol Tinker and John Solt.

Ikuko Atsumi would like to dedicate the book to Hualing Nieh Engle and Paul Engle and Kaoru Atsumi.

CLASSIC POETS

Princess Nukada

(7th Century)

Longing for you,
loving you,
waiting for you,
the bamboo blinds were swayed
only by the autumn wind.

At Nigitazu we wait for the moon
to put out to sea with our boats.
The moon comes and the tide rises.
Let us set to sea!

Does that bird
think of bygone times
as it flies singing
over the spring by the tree
of "exchange-deed leaves"?

As we pass through the field of purple herbs
fragrant with madder dye
across the Imperial game reserve
won't the guards see
you wave your sleeves to me?

PRINCESS NUKADA

*When the Emperor Tenji ordered
Fujiwara Kamatari to judge between
the beauty of cherry blossoms and the
red autumn leaves on the hills,
Princess Nukada gave judgment with
this poem*

When spring escapes
freed from being huddled in winter's sleep,
the birds that had been stilled
burst into song.
The buds that had been hidden
burst into flower.
The mountains are so thickly forested
that we cannot reach the flowers
and the flowers are so tangled with vines
that we cannot pick them.
When the maple leaves turn scarlet
on the autumn hills,
it is easy to gather them
and enjoy them.
We sigh over the green leaves
but leave them as they are.
That is my only regret—
So I prefer the autumn hills.

PRINCESS NUKADA

Empress Jitō

(645–702)

THE SUDDEN APPEARANCE OF CHERRY BLOSSOMS

Spring has passed
and it seems as if summer had come,
and pure white cloth is spread to dry
on the slopes of Heavenly Perfume Hill

ON THE DEATH OF THE EMPEROR TEMMU

Over North Mountain
dark clouds rise.
The stars go,
then the moon goes.

EMPRESS JITŌ

ON THE DEATH OF THE EMPEROR TEMMU

Even flaming fire
can be snatched up, smothered
and carried in a bag.
Why then can't I
meet my dead lord again?

EMPRESS JITŌ

The stars pass.
The moon passes.
Blue clouds pass above the mountains to the
    north.
The years go by.

EMPRESS JITŌ

Ōtomo no Sakanoe no Iratsume

(8th Century)

The orange tree
we planted in my garden
as a symbol of our love,
though we have come to regret it, our love
was worth doing.

I swore not to love you,
but my heart is as changeable
as cloth of hanezu dye.

                    ŌTOMO NO SAKANOE NO IRATSUME

I gave the jewel away to its owner.
Now we two sleep together,
I and my pillow.

ŌTOMO NO SAKANOE NO IRATSUME

My love hurts me because you cannot know
  it—
Love like the maiden lily,
blooming in the thickets of the summer moor.

ŌTOMO NO SAKANOE NO IRATSUME

Yosami, Wife of Hitomaro

(8th Century)

Day after day I've longed for my husband,
thinking each day he would return.
Now they tell me that he lies buried
in the canyon of Stone River.

You tell me not to long for you.
Since I do not know if we shall ever meet
   again,
how can I not live in anguish?

           YOSAMI, WIFE OF HITOMARO

We will never meet again face to face.
I pray that the clouds may rise over Stone
    River
So I can always see him in memory.

YOSAMI, WIFE OF HITOMARO

Lady Kii

(8th Century)

I know the reputation
of the idle ways
of the beach of Takashi.
I will not go near them,
for I would surely wet my sleeves.

Kasa no Iratsume

(8th Century)

The Gods of heaven are irrational.
So I may die and never meet you,
whom I love so much.

When evening comes
sorrow overwhelms my mind.
I see his phantom
that speaks the words
he used to say.

KASA NO IRATSUME

Evening comes and sorrow crowds my mind,
because your phantom always appears
speaking the old words in the old way.

KASA NO IRATSUME

Komachi

Doesn't he realize
that I am not
like the swaying kelp
in the surf,
where the seaweed gatherer
can come as often as he wants.

I fell asleep thinking of him,
and he came to me.
If I had known it was only a dream
I would never have awakened.

ONO NO KOMACHI

In the daytime
I can cope with them,
but when I see those jealous eyes
even in dreams,
it is more than I can bear.

ONO NO KOMACHI

Although I come to you constantly
over the roads of dreams,
those nights of love
are not worth one waking touch of you.

ONO NO KOMACHI

He does not come.
Tonight in the dark of the moon
I wake wanting him.
My breasts heave and blaze.
My heart chars.

ONO NO KOMACHI

Without changing color
in the emptiness
of this world of ours,
the heart of man
fades like a flower.

ONO NO KOMACHI

The colors of the flowers fade
as the long rains fall,
as lost in thought,
I grow older.

ONO NO KOMACHI

See page 72

Lady Ise

(9th–10th Century)

Since "the pillow knows all"
we slept without a pillow.
Still my reputation
reaches to the skies
like a dust storm.

Is it your command
that we must pass through this life,
never meeting again,
even for a space as short as the nodes
of the reeds of Naniwa?

LADY ISE

Even in dreams
I do not want him to know
that it is me he is making love to,
for I am overcome with blushes
when I see my face in my morning mirror.

LADY ISE

As the first spring mists appear
the wild geese leave.
Are they accustomed to live
in a flowerless land?

LADY ISE

Shall I come to see
plum blossoms in every stream
and wet my sleeves
in unpluckable water
as I do now?

LADY ISE

Shirome

(10th Century)

If I were only sure
I could live as long as I wanted to,
I would not have to weep
at parting from you.

kon

)

I am forgotten now.
I do not care about myself,
but I pity him
for the oaths he swore,
and his forsworn life.

Murasaki Shikibu

(974–1031)

This life of ours would not cause you sorrow
if you thought of it as like
the mountain cherry blossoms
which bloom and fade in a day.

I feel of others' affairs
as though they were
the water birds I watch
floating idly on the water.
My idleness comes
only from sorrow.

MURASAKI SHIKIBU

From the North send a message
on the wings of the wild geese,
written again and again
by their flight across the clouds.

MURASAKI SHIKIBU

FROM *THE TALE OF GENJI*

Lady Murasaki says:

The troubled waters
are frozen fast.
Under clear heaven
moonlight and shadow
ebb and flow.

Answered by Prince Genji:

The memories of long love
gather like drifting snow.
poignant as the mandarin ducks
who float side by side in sleep.

MURASAKI SHIKIBU

Akazome Emon

(?–1027)

In my heart's depth
I keep our secret smothered
although this morning I suffer
like a snipe scratching its feathers.

I can no longer tell dream from reality.
Into what world shall I awake
from this bewildering dream?

AKAZOME EMON

I, who cut off my sorrows
like a woodcutter,
should spend my life in the mountains.
Why do I still long
for the floating world?

AKAZOME EMON

It would have been better that I slept
the whole night through
without waiting for him,
than to have watched
until the setting of the moon.

AKAZOME EMON

Sei Shōnagon

(10th Century)

Since our relations
are like the crumbling
of Mount Imo and Mount Se,
they, like the Yoshino River
in that ravine
shall never flow smoothly again.

Mother of Michitsuna

(10th Century)

Sighing, sleeping alone all night,
do you realize how long the dawn is in
  coming?

Whenever the wind blows
I try to question it,
although it has obliterated
the spider's web against the sky.

MOTHER OF MICHITSUNA

Is our love over?
If only I could ask of your phantom
reflected on the surface
of the pond we made
as a symbol of our love—
but the surface is covered with duckweed.

MOTHER OF MICHITSUNA

Daini no Sanmi

(The Daughter of Murasaki)
(10th–11th Century)

From Mt. Arima,
over the bamboo plains of Ina,
the wind blows
rustling the leaves.
How shall I ever forget him?

Izumi Shikibu

(11th Century)

At the Sutra chanting of her dead daughter

In love longing
I listen to the monk's bell.
I will never forget you
even for an interval
short as those between the bell notes.

Another cruel letter today.
But I keep my heart burning
like a moxa made from
the very herbs of Mt. Ibuki.

IZUMI SHIKIBU

The pillow that knows all
won't tell, for it doesn't know,
and don't you tell
of our dream of a spring night.

IZUMI SHIKIBU

Soon I shall cease to be.
When I am beyond this world,
can I have the memory
of just one more meeting?

IZUMI SHIKIBU

Out of the darkness
on a dark path,
I now set out.
Shine on me,
moon of the mountain edge.

IZUMI SHIKIBU

Ise Tayū

(11th Century)

In Nara, the ancient capital,
the eight-fold cherry blossoms
bloom today,
and fill the nine-fold palace
with their perfume.

The farmer's clothes are soaked through and
    never dried,
in the long May rains
that fall without cease,
from a sky with never a rift in the clouds.

ISE TAYŪ

It is already so late at night
for our meeting,
but it is melancholy not to pause
at the ford of Saho
to listen to the plovers crying.

ISE TAYŪ

The clear water of the imperial pond
has been transparent for so many generations
that every water plant at the bottom can be
   recognized.
Just so, I am grateful to be singled out though
   I am of low birth.

ISE TAYŪ

Only the waning morning moon
visits my garden
where no lover comes.

ISE TAYŪ

*On receiving the gift of a robe with a
pattern of mingled plum blossoms
and chrysanthemums*

I thought the chrysanthemum bloomed in
    autumn
and the plum in spring.
Now I see
they are flowers of one season.

ISE TAYŪ

Today is the anniversary of our parting
and I long in sorrow
for you who will never return.

ISE TAYŪ

Unable to sleep,
I gaze at the flowers of the bush clover,
as the dew forms on them from the long night,
till suddenly before dawn
they are scattered by the wind.

ISE TAYŪ

Lady Sagami

(11th Century)

There is no night
when the lightning does not flash,
but where now is the mirage
which I saw so faintly?

With hate and misery
my sleeves are never dry.
How sad it is
that my name has been ruined by our love.

LADY SAGAMI

Lady Suwō

(11th–12th Century)

Pillowed on your arm
only for the dream of a spring night,
I have become the subject of gossip,
although nothing happened.

Princess Shikishi

(?–1201)

Life, like a thread piercing through jewels,
if you must break,
break now!
If I live any longer
I will weaken and show my hidden love.

I slept in the past,
that will never come back,
as though it was the present.
Around my pillow in my dreams
the perfume of orange blossoms floated,
like the fragrance of the sleeves
of the man who is gone.

PRINCESS SHIKISHI

Kenrei Mon-in Ukyō no Daibu

(12th Century)

The leaves of the bush clover rustle in the
   wind.
I, not a leaf,
watched you without a sound.
You may have thought I paid no attention.

My heart, like my clothing
is saturated with your fragrance.
Your vows of fidelity
were made to our pillow and not to me.

KENREI MON-IN UKYŌ NO DAIBU

I was sure I would never get lost
in the tangled roads of love.
Now I have been caught
in the karma of past lives.

KENREI MON-IN UKYŌ NO DAIBU

Giō

(12th Century)

The sprouting grass waiting for spring,
and the grass that begins to wither, were once
   the same
wild grass of the moor.
Sooner or later
they surely meet with autumn
and end in the season of weariness.

Yokobue

(Flute Player)
(12th Century)

How can I complain
that you have shaved your hair?
Since I can never again
pull your heartstrings
like a catalpa wood bow,
I have become a nun
following your Way.

Shizuka

(The dancing-girl mistress of Yoshitsune)
(12th Century)

How I long for the man who climbed Mt.
  Yoshino
plunging through the white snow
lying thick on its heights.

Lady Horikawa

(12th Century)

How long will it last?
I do not know
his heart.
This morning my thoughts are as tangled with
    anxiety
as my black hair.

The Daughter of Minamoto no Toshitaka

(12th Century)

For the sake of a night of a little sleep
by Naniwa bay,
must I live on longing for him,
exhausting my flesh?

Shunzei's Daughter

(1171?–1252?)

The wind blows through
the little hut in the rice field
and the moonlight shines through the roof
and guards us all through the night.

How can I blame the cherry blossoms
for rejecting this floating world
and drifting away as the wind calls them?

SHUNZEI'S DAUGHTER

As the season changes,
I change my clothes
to clothes dyed the color of cherry blossoms
which will fade as easily
from the hearts of men.

SHUNZEI'S DAUGHTER

It is unreasonable to ask my tears
to bear the sorrow of autumn,
as the light changes
the color even of the cinnamon tree in the
    moon
to red and yellow.

SHUNZEI'S DAUGHTER

Abutsu-Ni

(1209–1283)

Who knows
that in the depth of the ravine
of the mountain of my hidden heart
a firefly of my love is aflame.

HAIKU POETS
of the
TOKUGAWA PERIOD

Kawai Chigetsu-Ni

(1632–1736)

Grasshoppers
Chirping in the sleeves
Of a scarecrow.

Cats making love in the temple
But people would blame
A man and wife for mating in such a place.

KAWAI CHIGETSU-NI

Sute-Jo

(1633–1698)

A snowy morning
Everywhere II, II, II (two, two, two)
The tracks of clogs.

On the road through the clouds
Is there a short cut
To the summer moon?

DEN SUTE-JO

Ōme Shūshiki

(1668–1725)

Be careful! Be careful!
Of the cherry tree by the well
You're drunk with sake!

Chine-Jo

(Late 17th Century)

The fireflies' light.
How easily it goes on
How easily it goes out again.

Fukuda Chiyo-Ni

(1703–1775)

My hunter of dragonflies,
How far
has he wandered today?

"Cuckoo!"
"Cuckoo!"
While I meditated
on that theme
day dawned.

FUKUDA CHIYO-NI

See! The gleam
on my fishing line
of the summer moon.

FUKUDA CHIYO-NI

I forgot that my lips
were rouged,
drinking
of the clear spring water.

FUKUDA CHIYO-NI

Ukihashi

(Late 17th Century)

Whether I sit or lie
My empty mosquito net
Is too large.

Enomoto Seifu-Jo

(1731–1814)

Everyone is asleep
There is nothing to come between
the moon and me.

Matsumoto Koyū-Ni

(Late 18th Century)

At Ichiyiama
Boating on Lake Nio
The moon and fireflies
To the right and left.

Imaizumi Sogetsu-Ni

(?–1804)

How beautiful the Buddhist statues
At Saga
Half hidden in falling leaves.

Tagami Kikusha-Ni

(1752–1826)

The wind from Mt. Fuji

There is nothing like the cool
of the wind in this place
Blowing down from Mt. Fuji.

MODERN
TANKA POETS

Yosano Akiko

(1878–1942)

I can give myself to her
In her dreams
Whispering her own poems
In her ear as she sleeps beside me.

Without a word
Without a demand
A man and two women
Bowed and parted company
On the sixth of the month.

YOSANO AKIKO

Last autumn
The three of us tossed acorns
To the scattering carp.
Now in the cold morning wind off the pond
He and I stand hand in chilling hand.

YOSANO AKIKO

I remember the days
When the lily
Brilliant white
Was queen of the summer fields.

YOSANO AKIKO

A bird comes
delicately as a little girl
to bathe
in the shade of my tree
in an autumn puddle.

YOSANO AKIKO

I have the delusion
that you are with me
as I walk through the fields
of flowers, under the moon.

YOSANO AKIKO

Purple butterflies
fly at night through my dreams.
Butterflies, tell me,
have you seen in my village
the falling flowers of the wisteria?

YOSANO AKIKO

Is it because you always hope, my heart,
that I always light a lamp
in the orange twilight?

YOSANO AKIKO

My heart is like the sun,
drowned in darkness,
soaked with rain,
beaten by the winds.

YOSANO AKIKO

Sweet and sad
like love overwhelmed
with long sighs,
out of the depths of the willow
little by little
the moon appears.

YOSANO AKIKO

She who carries
in her heart a love
she knows must be unhappy,
overcast with storm clouds,
will never see their end
under the vast skies.

YOSANO AKIKO

Yamakawa Tomiko

(1879–1909)

The white roses I tried to braid in my hair
have all fallen
around my pillow of sickness.

I leave all the scarlet flowers
For the woman I love
And hiding my tears from her
I pick
The flower of forgetfulness.

YAMAKAWA TOMIKO

Chino Masako

(1880–1946)

I shall hide myself
within the moon of the spring night,
after I have dared to reveal
my love to you.

Kujō Takeko

(1887–1928)

I do not consider myself worth counting,
but sometimes even for me
heaven and earth are too small.

*new
vision*

moto Kanoko

(889–1939)

All day long having
buried himself
in the peonies,
the golden bee's
belly is swollen.

Gotō Miyoko

(1898–)

Gay colors flow
down streets that swirl
with dressed up girls
as winter comes on.

new topic

I listen to the pulse of a life
different from mine
in my womb,
and with it I can hear my own lonely heart.

GOTŌ MIYOKO

Scattered petals gather on the road,
more colorful than the blossoms on the
  branches.

Silently
time passes.
The only life I have
submits to its power.

HATSUI SHIZUE

see page 16

Anryū Suharu

(1923–)

When, with breaking heart,
I realize
this world is only a dream,
the oak tree looks radiant.

Baba Akiko

(1928–)

Since I don't know my mother,
I won't be a mother.
Facing the sun
we smile at each other,
myself and a faceless child.

In the autumn when words sound
like the echo of a stone ax,
some demon in me
wants to rise up and walk away.

BABA AKIKO

Punished in the moment of love
I looked back
and saw the jealousy of the Gods
overflow the Milky Way.

BABA AKIKO

MODERN
HAIKU POETS

Sugita Hisajo

(1890–1946)

O flower garment!
When I take it off,
various strings coil around me.

Mending his broken *tabi*
without becoming a Nora
I am a teacher's wife.

SUGITA HISAJO

Mitsuhashi Takajo

(1899–1972)

O bird's singing!
The dead walk
on the plain of the sea.

The hair ornament of the sun
has sunk
into the legendary sea.

MITSUHASHI TAKAJO

Hashimoto Takako

(1899–1963)

Towards the starry sky,
apples go flooding
from the pile.

Nakamura Teijo

(1900–)

The season of changing clothes
For summer; I see a bridge
not so far away.

Hoshino Tatsuko

(1903–)

O brightness
of peony's buds
softly splitting open!

Yagi Mikajo

(1924–)

The genitals of woods
in full bloom;
its gills are breathing.

A marathon runner's legs
fan in and out.
Are they the disciples of a waterfall?

YAGI MIKAJO

FREE VERSE
POETS

Yosano Akiko

(1878–1942)

LABOR PAINS

I am sick today,
sick in my body,
eyes wide open, silent,
I lie on the bed of childbirth.

Why do I,
so used to the nearness of death,
to pain and blood and screaming,
now uncontrollably tremble with dread?

A nice young doctor tried to comfort me,
and talked about the joy of giving birth.
Since I know better than he about this matter,
what good purpose can his prattle serve?

Knowledge is not reality.
Experience belongs to the past.
Let those who lack immediacy be silent.
Let observers be content to observe.

I am all alone,
totally, utterly, entirely on my own,
gnawing my lips, holding my body rigid,
waiting on inexorable fate.

There is only one truth.
I shall give birth to a child,
truth driving outward from my inwardness.
Neither good nor bad; real, no sham about it.

With the first labor pains,
suddenly the sun goes pale.
The indifferent world goes strangely calm.
I am alone.
It is alone I am.

Fukao Sumako

(1893–1974)

✓ BRIGHT HOUSE

It is a bright house;
not a single room is dim.

It is a house which rises high
on the cliffs, open
as a lookout tower.

When the night comes
I put a light in it,
a light larger than the sun and the moon.

Think
how my heart leaps
when my trembling fingers
strike a match in the evening.

I lift my breasts
and inhale and exhale the sound of love
like the passionate daughter of a lighthouse
    keeper.

It is a bright house.
I will create in it
a world no man can ever build.

Hayashi Fumiko

(1904–1951)

THE LORD BUDDHA

I fell in love with the Lord Buddha
when I kiss his chill lips sacrilegiously
my heart swoons

from beginning to end
my peaceful blood flows backward
overcome with sacrilegiousness
my heart has been overwhelmed
by the beauty
of his irresistible perfect peace
oh Lord Buddha

Nagase Kiyoko

(1906–)

MOTHER

I am always aware of my mother,
ominous, threatening,
a pain in the depths of my consciousness.
My mother is like a shell,
so easily broken.
Yet the fact that I was born
bearing my mother's shadow
cannot be changed.
She is like a cherished, bitter dream
my nerves cannot forget
even after I awake.
She prevents all freedom of movement.
If I move she quickly breaks,
and the splinters stab me.

Nakamura Chio

(1913–)

A DIARY WITHOUT DATES

I, no sense of being alive,
live next door to death.

My neck was so feeble,
it toppled if anyone touched it.
I felt I had turned to stone.

Every day my anxiety grew deeper,
until it enveloped me so thickly
that I could see nothing.
Alone in an illimitable desert
I wept hopelessly, as if in a nightmare in
    dawn
where the open mouthed blue sky wept
    with me.

The trees wept,
a bird's body,
a horse's bleached bones,
all spell bound.
Immobile, watched with bated breath
the figure of death.

The world was unbearably still.
I sat side by side with death,
held immobile in reality,
only hoping I would not fall.

Takada Toshiko

(1916–)

THE SEACOAST AT MERA

One day this summer,
I swam on the seacoast at Mera,
off the point of Bōsō peninsula.
Bathing at the edge of the rocks
with no shadow of other people near me,
the surf washed my body smooth
and made it flush all over.
When I took off my swimsuit
in the shadow of the rocks and dried myself
my summer had ended.
On my way back along the steep trail,
I looked back casually and found around the
    rocky point
four or five women divers standing in the surf
and only the summer day from which I was
    stealing away
shining above them.

Takiguchi Masako

(1933–)

SLAUGHTERHOUSE

Blood gushes out of the throat
of a cow hung upside down:
za ah ah ah—
With sucking sounds as it gushes
over the blood stained concrete floor,
the cold profile of a woman
is superimposed.

> Wrapping a crimson *obi*
> tightly around her waist
> she plucks out her life root
> nothing but matter remains.

The moment the man's hand touches the
    eyelid
the legs drop and spread
with a horrible speed
and then slowly the trembling
legs form a half circle.
Four hundred cows make half circles every
    day.

Sliding along the rail on the ceiling
the meat lands heavily on its shoulder:
Bang—
In the elasticity of the thick fat
in the smell of blood
the being of love and sorrow is lost.
Love lost lovers who have lost life
greet and make love.

Waiting in the slaughterhouse
the sunset exposed itself
and the steers copulated.

BLUE HORSE

Sunken murmurs rise from the sea bottom
Where you can see a horse through a trough
   of the waves,
Blind in both eyes,
a blue horse plodding along the sea bottom.
The memory of men on its back almost gone.
How long has this horse lived in the sea?
Is the blood splashed on its back its own?
If not, whose was it?
It plods on, imperturbably
Brushing aside the clinging seaweed with its
   forelegs
Its blind eyes stealthily turn
To an indigo deeper far and lonelier than the
   sea.
Blood oozes from its wounded belly in the
   wash of the sea
And is carried away from wave to wave.

When autumn comes
A cold thick fog rises from the sea.
At that time the horse crouches alone
Its legs folded under it
In the shadow of the rocks at the bottom of
   the sea
Enduring the cold.
Enduring.
Waiting.

TAKIGUCHI MASAKO

Mitsui Futabako

(1919–)

GRAZING

There is a peaceful little community
in a place of burned up hopes,
beside the tracks of dreams
      that drifted away,
  on the edge of a village
      where crowds pass by.

There, men gather in harmony
    to graze like sheep and fawns.

On all the beautiful flowers
a sun comes and goes
    through the clouds in freedom.

Rin

SHELLFISH

I wake at midnight.
The little shellfish I bought last evening
are alive with their mouths slightly open.

I will eat them all when day breaks.

I laugh a hag's laugh.
Afterwards there is nothing left of the night,
except to sleep with my mouth slightly open.

WALKING - WITH - A - CANE - PASS

I visited my distant relatives
by Lake Suwa in Shinshū.

The old woman whom I had not seen for a
   long time
was lying down quietly
unable to talk.

She showed the rise and fall of the long years
when she had raised eight children
and at last became
like the two small curves of the mountain.
In the valley of her buttocks
fell a round lump steaming with life.

When I climbed to the height of
   Walking-With-A-Cane-Pass
I looked out over the entire Yatsugatake
   Mountain Range
and beyond that, the snow covered mountains
   stretched away.

I don't know why, but my hand knew
the coldness of white underwear
changed for winter
and the warmth of skin bared at the neck.
Fine, bare trees stood like downy hair,
clouds poured out of a ravine.

I was compelled to stand there
as on an observation platform
looking out over two kinds of nature
under the bright sky,
I endured it, holding my nose
at what was great and beautiful.

ISHIGAKI RIN

Shindō Chie

(1920–)

SPACE

Who could know in advance
the slight curve of the line
of the flower about to bloom in the midst of
    the sky,
taking its position in the midst of abundant
    time?

Who could decide in advance
the form and the subtle color
of the flower about to open to its extremity,
devoting itself to abundant golden time?

Breezes play,
only sunlight knows
it is being robbed.

The blue in the sky inclines
to the limits of its flow.
The sky sways
as the petals wave.

Ibaragi Noriko

(1926–   )

DIALOGUE

I stand still under an orange tree,
in the heavy perfume of the white flowers.
Regulus, the chief star of the Lion, twinkles
like a cool young man talking to the flowers.

I witness this strange exchange of courtesies
between the will powers of heaven and earth.
A beautiful shudder runs over me—

A girl left out in her air raid hood
while the siren of the nearby village
kept on blowing.

No jealousy so deep has ever come over me
I learned the habit of dialogue that night.

WHAT A LITTLE GIRL
HAD ON HER MIND

What a little girl had on her mind was:
Why do the shoulders of other men's wives
give off so strong a smell like magnolia;
or like gardenias?
What is it,
that faint veil of mist,
over the shoulders of other men's wives?
She wanted to have one,
that wonderful thing
even the prettiest virgin cannot have.

The little girl grew up.
She became a wife and then a mother.
One day she suddenly realized;
the tenderness
that gathers over the shoulders of wives,
is only fatigue
from loving others day after day.

IBARAGI NORIKO

Fukunaka Tomoko

(1928–   )

IT'S NOT THE SAME

The demonstrators who filled the streets of
    Seoul
from the night of January 21
to the dawn of the 22nd
1968
and the suicide core
of the Vietcong
who attacked Saigon and besieged the
    American embassy
at dawn January 30
1968
And
the students who charged against the riot
    staves of the police
to close Sasebo Harbor
January 19
1968
They weren't the same people.

The guerrillas in Seoul
were not the invading North Korean army,
the suicide core in Saigon were not the North
    Vietnam army
and
those students who broke into the American
    air base
at Sasebo over the chain link fence,
drenched by water cannon,
what happened to all those people after that?

Nothing is ever quite the same
each time is different from every other
the heart of each person is disconnected.
But if there is one thing
that is the same,
it is that neither the newspapers nor
  television
ever reported on those young men after that.
And
the enemy in the world today
is not the United States,
is not the Soviet Union
but, bridged between you and me
unidentifiable
words of silence.

Fukui Hisako

(1929–)

NOW IS THE TIME

Now is the time
Oh Bird!
This is the season fruits grow from the depths
    of the earth.
This is the time that their ripened aim presses
    to the sky
brushing the snow from their wings
beyond that vague white phenomenon
lies a world of ripe red fruit
which can't be picked
and which refuses the combinations of the
    puzzle.

Can your flapping and twittering
narrow the white spaces?
Oh bird!
Is this the first time you became aware your
    body was white
Did you ever wish
to become like ether
or to become a frozen will following its own
    track
oblivious of effort in infinite space?
Is there still
time left
to include
the passion for fruition.

Oh bird!
fly!
chatter with your strange loud voice
and turn into a frenzied *ashura*
stripping the fruit from the tree.

Shinkawa Kazue

(1929-)

AN EVENT WHICH MAKES
NO NEWS

Did you see in the shadowy woods
a branch grew, leaves came out
of a girl's pliant extended arms
and quickly became a tree?
Did you see?
A youth stood by the tree,
took off his deep blue coat,
and in a moment became a dove?

(The telephone keeps ringing, ringing.
   Nobody answers, nobody is there, today is
   Sunday)

When the lights go on on the suburban trains,
People come back to their office buildings
wearing the face of human beings.

Haven't you heard the story?
In the nearby meadow,
one or two unknown horses have lingered on
these days after a holiday.

(The telephone keeps ringing, ringing.
   Nobody answers.
Nobody is there. Eventually it's Monday)

Inoue Michiko

(?–)

GET ANGRY, COMPASS

Sweat begins to ooze from Compass's
    forehead
Damn the theater owner!
Do you mean to say my right foot has no
    joint?

When I call "Lower the percussion!"
they buried it in the ground.
I can't land on my left foot it's too dangerous.
And the dancers in the ritual
refuse to come out.

The premiere danseuse was the wife of the
    theater owner
who descended from the flies with the wheel
    of bondage on both arms.
She waves on the crowd of dancers from both
    wings,
her lips trembling.

I can't even walk!
Hold on to my shoulders
quick!
Compass stand motionless
his right foot stuck in his ear.

Tada Chimako

(1930–)

MIRROR

My mirror is always a little taller than I am.
It laughs a little later than I laugh.
I blush like a boiled crab,
and cut off a projection of myself with my nail
    scissors.

When I let my lips approach the mirror,
it blurs, and I vanish beyond my sighs,
as a nobleman disappears behind his crest,
and a blackguard behind his tattoo.

My mirror is the cemetery of smiles.
Traveler, when you come to Lakaidaimon,
tell them that there stands here a grave,
painted white with heavy makeup,
with only wind blowing in the mirror.

shi Kazuko

(-)

THE ANNIVERSARY OF SAMANSA'S DEATH

With her head swinging like a white lily,
A devilish girl who had been dancing to Mary
   Wells' music,
Samansa, a woman behind a Noh mask,
Dropped dead.

"On the thirteenth of last August,
Coming back to the night from swimming in
   the sea,
I became unsteady and felt as if I was half in
   a dream.
I realized that I had slept in a casket
When I came to myself in her room.
I wonder, is it too young to die, only 25 years
   old?
I wonder, will there be gay bars in the other
   world?
There must be lots of gay angels.
I wonder, maybe I would prefer hell.
How troublesome it all is!
I don't give a damn!
Under roses crimson as blood,
I want to sleep for a while,
Perhaps forever."

"On the roof of the beer garden,
'CLOSED IN CASE OF RAIN'
From 5:30 to 9 p.m. two thousand yen,
My face shining in the neon lights
Like a malignant ghost's,
I go-go dance in the Spring evening.
It was long ago, that evening in Spring,
About the time when I was still alive.
I love Marlene Dietrich and burn an incense
    stick to her picture,
In the fragrance of roses.
To the music, "Two Lovers," by Mary Wells.
After all, I have never had a lover,
In this world neither a heterosexual man nor
    a homosexual woman,
I have lived between one world and another
    world.
I've just been an invocation to Buddha.
This is the anniversary of my death in an
    ecstacy,
Every day since I have been alive.
It shouldn't be like this.
But the fact is, that people exist who think of
    the anniversary
of their deaths as their hobbies.
Tomorrow is supposed to be the anniversary
    of my death,
Tomorrow I am supposed to have been
    alive—once upon a time."

I FIRE AT THE FACE OF THE
COUNTRY WHERE I WAS BORN

I fire at the face
Of the country where I was born,
At the glazed forehead,
At the sea birds perched,
On that forehead—
Vancouver, beautiful city,
I shoot you because I love you.
Gasoline city, neither one thing nor another.
Neither
A prisoners' ward—without bars,
Nor the loneliness excreted
By lonely youth
I wish it could be
a liberation ward,
a liberation ward, where petals of free thighs
    dance in the sky,
a freedom ward,
a happiness ward,
a goddamn it ward,
a goddamn it divine ward,
a profanation ward,
a devil's marriage ward,
a rich diet ward,
a senior citizen's lasciviousness ward,
a wanton woman ward,
a handsome boy ward,
a homosexual ward,
a wanderer's ward,
In the morning of this beautiful city,
With beautiful Lion Head Mountain,
Covered with snow,
In the deep blue sky that soaks
Into the back of my eyes,

I find myself washing my face and teeth
In front of the washing bowl.
It's so sanitary—
A toothbrush and toothpaste kind of purity.
There is not a single bacterium in this
    country.
Not even that little tiny bacterium
Which the Devil called the soul can grow.
It doesn't exist.
All of them,
The King named Old Morality,
The people in power,
Who clothed the honest citizen
And named him Unseen Conservative,
Who stands at the bus stops—
One of them is a platinum blonde girl
Two of them are old women on pensions.
But nobody knows that the story
Of the beautiful girl who sleeps in the forest
Is about Vancouver.
No one knows that this beautiful city
Is the model for that beauty.
Victoria Vancouver, a girl,
A beautiful girl slowly coming towards me
Who opens her eyes but stays asleep
And comes to me smiling
A diplomatic smile.
I aim at the face of this country
Where I was born, and at the seabirds
Perched on the sleepwalker's forehead.
And then,
As the waves splash, moment by moment,
I stand ready to fire
With the pistol of confession.

SHIRAISHI KAZUKO

A CHINESE ULYSSES

Turning back, he found no face,
No newborn face of his own.
Face is a country,
And his country was won away by red
   thoughts.
No longer with a face,
And with no lips to kiss,
He moves on.

His native land is under an unfamiliar map.
Only his mother's womb
Is the sign of a passport from his country of
   birth.
He fumbles for a name.
He left his country.
He is Ulysses
Who knows no return—
Ulysses barred from returning—
Ulysses who has no possible date of
   returning.
Holding wife, children, and flowers,
Burning a torch of poetry,
He cries toward the open sea,
"Is anybody there?"
Any faces proving he really exists?
A thousand, a million, a billion changing
   forms
Make love with the night sea and the stars
   falling on the waves
He enters their music
Seeking his interior country.
He joins the ascetics of love making
Though he can create thousands,
Tens of thousands, of his descendants' faces,

He'll never meet
Nor touch
The face of his newborn country.
So today,
Today again,
Ulysses
Crosses the sea and reaches land.
In a cold country town of Midwest America.
He enters a building
At two in the afternoon.
Nobody
Pays any attention to him.
He is neither a personal attendant to the
    President,
Nor a gangster with a revolver,
Nor a muscle-bound world champion boxer.
He is tall and beautiful with a straight nose,
And he carries a hidden dignity and fire,
But has no other characteristics.
So unless he is violent
Or wears medals of honor
People will just pass him by
Because philosophy is an invisible living
    thing.
Nowadays people aren't scared of ghosts,
Especially living ghosts,
So he goes unnoticed for thousands of years.
He never dies.
He is not allowed to die.
He is Ulysses
A living myth.

"I feel wonderful today!"
He tells me while drunk.
But can he really feel drunk,
Can he get drunk in the sea of liquor
Listening to Sirens?

Would he know a Siren?
The Siren's voice changes to Elvis.
Is Presley a Siren?
Can a record from the rock 'n roll age
Carry him to Penelope?
He talks about a man who went to India,
A man named Snyder in search of
   self-realization.
He talks of the art of living freely.
He thinks of it as eating a rainbow,
As making love with a rainbow.
He hopes to grasp the far away clouds,
And
The Siren
Goes to bed unfucked
Listening to Elvis' record.

He gets up in the morning,
Returns from lunch,
Is about to go to bed at night, and discovers,
No face in the mirror nor in the bedroom.
Suddenly he realizes
He is Ulysses.
Still he can't go home.
He can't go home.
He has no country to return to,
Always moving on.

Blues
Reaches my ears
From the lonely country of a nameless man.
Beyond Dixieland Jazz
It goes back thousands of years
To the first baby's first bath.

SHIRAISHI KAZUKO

THE MAN ROOT
For Sumiko's Birthday

God if he exists
Or if he doesn't
Still has a sense of humor
Like a certain type of man

So this time
He brings a gigantic man root
To join the picnic
Above the end of the sky of my dreams
Meanwhile
I'm sorry
I didn't give Sumiko anything for her birthday
But now I wish I could at least
Set the seeds of that God given penis
In the thin, small, and very charming voice of
    Sumiko
On the end of the line

Sumiko, I'm so sorry
But the penis shooting up day by day
Flourishes in the heart of the galaxy
As rigid as a wrecked bus
So that if
You'd like to see
The beautiful sky with all its stars
Or just another man instead of this God given
    cock
A man speeding along a highway
With a hot girl
You'll have to hang
All the way out of the bus window
With your eyes peeled

It's spectacular when the cock
Starts nuzzling the edge of the cosmos
At this time
Dear Sumiko
The lonely way the stars of night shine
And the curious coldness of noon
Penetrates my gut
Seen whole
Or even if you refused to look
You'd go crazy
Because you can trace
The nameless, impersonal and timeless penis
In the raucous atmosphere
Of the passers-by
That parade it in a portable shrine
In that stir of voices
You can hear an immensity of savage
Rebellion, the curses of
Heathen gism
Sometimes
God is in conference or out to lunch
It seems he's away
Absconding from debts but leaving his penis.

So now
The cock abandoned by God
Trots along
Young and gay
And full of callow confidence
Amazingly like the shadow
Of a sophisticated smile

The penis bursting out of bounds
And beyond measure
Arrives here

Truly unique and entirely alone
Seen from whatever perspective
It's faceless and speechless
I would like to give you, Sumiko
Something like this for your birthday

When it envelops your entire life
And you've become invisible even to yourself
Occasionally you'll turn into the will
Of exactly this penis
And wander
Ceaselessly
I want to catch in my arms
Forever
Someone like you

SHIRAISHI KAZUKO

Yoshihara Sachiko

(1932–)

CANDLE

Going
Gone
Don't be going
Be gone
Don't forgive
Forgive—

I am burning in the darkness
Hot wax drips along my sides
I am decreasing
But the blood I shed increases

For the sake of my small light
The surrounding darkness becomes thicker
I can't see you
I can't see the darkness in you

Because of my small light
I can't see myself
I can only see the white blood I shed

You pass through me, Darkness,
Not sideways but rising
In the opposite direction of my decreasing
Through the flame that I wanted
To slightly singe your fingertips
Now my flame barely flickers

In a quiet room my scorching makes a sound
My little fire is hot
It burns my hair my nails my eyes
To burn is
To vomit life because I've been gluttonous
Life melts into a puddle at my feet
Like repentance

I am consumed in flames alone
When I return to the darkness
The darkness returns to itself
You passed through me
Fire and darkness passed through me

What was consumed is not me
I am not the fire which burnt
To burn
And to be consumed, that is me

So I am here
Standing in the blood drained from me
I am here
Always, endlessly, I am here

Forgive me for burning
Forgive me for disappearing

RESURRECTION

To kill love so as not to commit suicide, that
    is self defense
The pistol levelled at you takes aim at my
    heart
With hot sin and cold punishment
I crack   from there I should break
Incredible hole   and then perhaps death
    will quietly spread
The dripping sounds of the world
    disappear   afterwards
In the long long solitary cell   they may be
An unquiet death   a burning
    death   burning life
Spider in the rain   wet with its own
    sweat   spinning a web
Gradually tapers and smears out   the oval
    shining zero

YOSHIHARA SACHIKO

BLASPHEMY

God   certainly   wasn't
sun stubbornly continued rising
i stubbornly continued loving

but God was there   one day
i took a look in myself

from around what time?
was it from the time i was a fish?
in my spirit   there was a deep wound
no sound   no color   without
   interval:heat
the flowing blood   resembled God

from the wound   i
felt everything   then
stubbornly   i did

those are my watery eyes   thirsty lips
a dog's sense of smell   deer's sense of
   hearing
that was   my sadness
sadness is   a mollusk's   two antennae

when the world meaninglessly flowed from
   the wound
i in the middle of trembling
there is a world   sky:blue
blue sky pierced   into wound

God stubbornly continued to be absent
i stubbornly continued loving

YOSHIHARA SACHIKO

I FORGET

when i awake
i wonder
if the color
i thought i saw
in my dream
was real
or imaginary

was it red?
i turn back
towards the word red
but the color is gone

what i thought was
being alive
is only various colors
reflected and
scattered
in my mind

sun setting
turned the windowpane orange
shower spray
was a diamond color
so i thought

now only the memory
of color remains
the window
and the shower spray
have vanished

YOSHIHARA SACHIKO

Kōra Rumiko

(1932–   )

WOMAN

It is a being somewhat like a well.
When you drop a well bucket
you will find
restlessness deep in the well.

The water is dark and soft
she has no boundaries anymore
she engraphs herself there

That she is herself
is more difficult than water is water
just as it's difficult for water to go beyond
   water
she and I are linked in mutual love
who once betrayed each other
two mirrors who reflected each other

When I escape from her, I incessantly
am forced to be her and when I confront her
instead I become *him*.

What I do is myself
When I didn't see what I did
it only means that I didn't do more.

Tomioka Taeko
(1935–)

GIRLFRIEND

The concubine next door
chants sutras.
In the early afternoon
I saw an animal like a donkey
pass under the window.
I saw it through the gap in the curtains.
There is a woman who comes to visit me,
always through the gap in the curtains.
Today she hasn't come yet.
She promised to come,
in her Viet Nam dress
of georgette crepe
with that walk
that makes all the men run after her.
She hasn't come;
maybe she's dead.
Before,
when I went traveling with her,
she wanted to buy an old woodcut
of Germany or somewhere
at an antique shop out in the country.

At a country inn,
for the first time I had a chance
to dishevel her hair
as thick as Bridgit Bardot's.
We danced
Viennese waltzes,
our crimson cheeks rubbing
as long as we wished
Sometimes she let fall
transparent optimistic poetry
that now I want to take for tears.
She hasn't come today.
I pray
out loud though it's only noon,
just like the concubine next door.
She
didn't promise not to come.
The one who goes.
Oh, the one who has gone.

Yoshiyuki Rie

(1939–)

SACRIFICIAL VICTIM

A beautiful person awakes
singing in the forest.
A dying bird
rests on my hand
like a fallen leaf.

Atsumi Ikuko

(1940–)

THE RING

Of the two kinds of wing-shaped rings on his
    desk
I point to the bigger one.
Then in silence
I get on the pedestal and open my legs.
Outside the window cherry blossoms are in
    full bloom.
Out of the cold buried between my thighs
Branches and leaves stretch themselves
And drop green fruit over my eyelids.
The sound of the doctor driving a screw
With skillful hands. When I bend myself back
Warm liquid oozes through my pipe.
Lying like this how often have I become an
    object?
Tonight I will sleep alone.
The zircon-inset ring you put on my finger
Already many years now
Inside my jewelry box
Has slept together with imitations.

DIFFERENT DIMENSIONS

What is it? Something sought by everyone?
Suddenly it splits me in two.

I feel free to walk anywhere,
at least for now. I stride over the distant past.

Some time ago, in a silence stronger
than soy beans popping in the pan.

Hope? Waiting for footsteps?
Perhaps to become a Heian court lady

surrounded by a screen of illusions
waiting for some prince?

Or is it the prayer of a wife in war-time,
anxious for her man in the field?

Don't say it rises like a spinning wheel
without hitting all the rungs.

Is it resolution? The blazing blue flame
of mothers secretly resisting their patriarchs?

But I can't get by on that alone.
Why not simply break out?

I only have to get the rhythm down
to fly through the day to day.

Like a pilot, astronaut
I too am in a capsule, though.

ATSUMI IKUKO

Kanai Mieko

(1947–)

IN THE TOWN WITH CAT-SHAPED MAZE

> —Even blue mold is
> A map of dream,
> Oh lunar park!

I waited in a map of dreams
and I found the town
was exactly as the map showed
a town covered with a thin seven colored
   membrane of oil
with a maze shaped like a big fluffy pliant cat
with transparent streets one on top of the
   other
on this side of the street along the beach
what does the unhurt dream once more melt
   into?
It melts into the map of the mesh of the blood
   vessels
throughout the body.
into the town of the cat shaped maze
harbor, amphitheatre, park, restaurant,
then an eternal voyager who will never return
then an eternal surveyor who will come
then a hyena

(It was in those days that I had a job in a
restaurant in a secluded alley at the base of
the cat's tail. A little ways away there was a
heart shaped park which the neighbors called
Cat's Balls Park but its polite name was Luna
Park I don't know why they called it that I
like the name Cat's Balls better. (Maybe
because there was such a marvelous view of

the moon from the park) Since he never came
back every day I broke a china beckoning-cat
into pieces throwing it on the floor of the
damp kitchen. (I agreed that they could
deduct the price of the cat from my pay) Each
time I did it the aged cook grinned and gave
me a donut. I picked up the pieces of cat and
ate the donut).

Over the faded park the sky drizzling rain lost
    the moon
from the spring showers to the monsoons
throw away the transparent sphere
it's only a childish ball game
nobody has ever survived
except as a fat ghost.

(So the old cook advised me out of his gentle
    wisdom)

In a white glass jar like an amphitheatre
my fingers scoop out cold cream
what is being torn off, my fingers or the
    cosmetics?
transparent grains conceal themselves in the
    essence of the cream
their small dull points make my blood spurt
and stream under the smooth hills of my
    fingers
a gush of magma of my scanty blood
my lips suck it up
dizziness for smallness

A mental compass constantly draws
    transparent circumferences
Sweeping up and down on the curved surface
    inside the sphere.

Its reality wears a sandal that is perhaps a full
  vision of the moon
The moon waning in the shape of a gentle
  inlet of a south sea island is his toenail
This is a land from which a sail hardly ever
  returns

Beware captain,
of the singing voices don't tie your body
to the going insane masts
don't be enraptured by the beatific death
in the whirlpool of transparent fruit juice
or the tornado of sand that reveals death
at the end of its wandering voyage
don't look. Don't forget the restaurant here in
  this country.

(So the old cook filled with mild sadness
  advised again)

In a restaurant in a secluded alley at the base
of the tail, in the town of the cat shaped maze,
I waited for him to come back to me. In their
comfortable cage in the park the bears
wandered around in their trousers, and the
hyena having just arrived from the South ran
as hard as he could on the road of night and
bit me on the shoulder and I waited
drinking off the pale white milk. But he did not
come back. I waited in the town of the maze
shaped like the cat and the town became
more and more transparent, and the harbor
became a bay where a drop of the cat's tears
calmed itself.

REVOLUTION

Since the images you demand
cling to me
I cannot form my own image.
I am forced to live
by your images,
I am always living like that,
so
I understand
revolution is really body aching.

REMORSE CAME SLOWLY

World,
it was long time ago that I first saw you
you passed by pretending
you didn't even know me
but what showed up was always you.
Now they say nobody's gone.
That's the situation.
So I decided to take steps
no love songs?
huh? (What in the world are you going to
    sing?
You can depend on it. Love songs will revive
    someday.) After all
I guess I won't sing for a while.
I'm sure people are lonely.
Maybe so, but
I've simply got to
take back
in a short time
the time I met you behind the time
the world hugely closed in on me

And remorse came slowly.

NISHI JUNKO

ANONYMOUS
GEISHA SONGS

I have prepared the hibachi
leveling the ashes
and there I have written my lover's name,
my eyes full of tears

Tonight as I sleep alone
I am on my bed of tears
like an abandoned boat
on the deep sea

When it's the man I love
he goes by and doesn't come in
but men I hate—
a hundred times a day

The loves of a little while ago
and the smoke of tobacco
little by little leave
only ashes

Before me
when I look into the mirror
the face of my lover
seems to come and go

The heavy sobs which rise up and choke me
I drive back
and in sake and tobacco I drown
my sorrow

You and me
we live inside an egg
me, I am the white
and wrap you round with my body

When I've got the blues
as deep as deep can be
I want to pass the rest of my life
as a nun

When I pour sake
for the man I love
even before he drinks up
I blush like a cherry blossom

What difference does it make
What other people say
for you my love grows and grows
without stopping

Listen I am just like
the cuckoo down the hillside
who sobs all night
that is our karma

From the dream where we made love
my laughter called me back
and I searched all around me
my eyes full of tears

Between Awajishima and Suma
the shorebirds come and go
all night troubling sleep
of the guards of Suma Gate

From the Isle of Awaji
each night there comes
to the apprenticed geishas
a pine wind for them to play with

I got up and opened the shoji
and looked out on the full moon night
but there was nothing there
but a cuckoo crying to himself

I.
Notes on the Poets

CLASSIC POETS

PRINCESS NUKADA lived in the latter half of the 7th Century. She was the daughter of Prince Kagami, wife and the favorite of the Emperor Temmu. She is considered to be the greatest of the women poets of the Ōmi period, the first section of the *Manyōshū Anthology*, the first collection of Japanese poetry.

EMPRESS JITŌ (645–702) was the wife of the Emperor Temmu and on his death in 686 she ascended the throne herself and ruled for ten years. The evidence is that the early Yamato people, from whom the historical royal family of Japan emerged, may have been one of the few examples of genuine matriarchy. The early empresses may well have been essentially shamanesses, the embodiment of the religious values of the clan. As time went on they became rarer and rarer as sole rulers.

OTOMO no SAKANOE no IRATSUME (8th Century) was a member of the then-powerful Ōtomo clan and is generally considered to be the leading woman poet of the early Nara Period. She was an aunt of the great poet Ōtomo no Yakamochi, to whom her daughter, also a poet, was married. In its brief period of dominance, about a hundred years, the Ōtomo clan produced almost as many poets as the Fujiwara family.

YOSAMI, WIFE OF HITOMARO (8th Century) was probably a girl from the village of Tsunu in Iwami, one of possibly three wives of Kakinomoto Hitomaro, who was the greatest poet of the *Manyōshū* and is generally considered to be the greatest of all Japanese poets. Their dates are indefinite but they are assumed to have lived around 700 A.D.

LADY KII (8th Century) was the consort of Prince Aki and one of the many lovers of Ōtomo no Yakamochi.

KASA no IRATSUME lived in the 8th Century and was one of the lovers of Ōtomo no Yakamochi. To modern tastes, she is the most moving of the women poets of the *Manyōshū*. The entranced eroticism of her poems to Yakamochi would be imitated by the great women poets of the 9th and 10th Centuries, notably Izumi Shikibu and Ono no Komachi.

ONO no KOMACHI (9th Century) is the legendary beauty of Japan. Her father was Yoshisada, Lord of Dewa. She is the central figure in three of the most profoundly moving Noh plays and is supposed to have died an ugly old beggar woman. This is almost certainly pure myth. Her beauty may be legendary but her rank as one of the greatest erotic poets in any language is not. Her poems begin the extreme verbal complexity which distinguishes the poetry of the *Kokinshū Anthology* from the presentational immediacy of the *Manyōshū*.
An alternate translation:

> The color of the flowers
> has faded
> while I contemplated it,
> as my body
> passed through the world.

LADY ISE was the daughter of Fujiwara no Tsugikage, Lord of Ise, later Lord of Yamato. She was the lover of Prince Atsuyoshi, by whom she bore a daughter, the poet Nakatsukasa. She later became a concubine of the Emperor Uda, to whom she bore Prince Yuki-Akari. She is to be distinguished from Ise Tayū, daughter of the Chief Priest of the Ise Shrines, and from the Priestess of Ise who had a brief love affair and an exchange of poems with the poet Narihara in the 10th Century. We are now well into the period of the great women writers of Japan, a group of women, roughly contemporary, unparalleled in world literature.

SHIROME (10th Century) was an *oiran,* a prostitute, not a geisha, and the only woman of any such position included in the Imperial Anthologies. Her poem is in the *Kokinshū,* purely on its great merits, which are more obvious in Japanese than in translation.

LADY UKON (10th Century) left no sign of her existence except her poetry.

MURASAKI SHIKIBU (974–1031) is Japan's greatest writer, the author of the *Genji Monogatari, The Tale of Genji,* probably the greatest novel ever written, and long antedating the appearance of the novel in the West or in China. Lady Murasaki was the great-granddaughter of the poet Fujiwara no Kanesuke, the daughter of Tametoki, Lord of Echigo, the wife of Fujiwara no Nobutaka, and the chief Maid of Honor for Sōshi, chief consort of the Emperor Ichijō. Her daughter, Daini no Sanmi, was also a poet. The translation of *The Tale of Genji* by Arthur Waley is itself one of the classics of 20th Century literature. She also left a diary and a collection of her poems and was one of the few women to write poetry in Chinese. The greatness of the novel tends to overshadow her poetry, but the novel contains hundreds of poems, many of them of great beauty, and some essential to the development of the extraordinarily complex psychology of the plot. The two poems from *The Tale of Genji* are the pivot of the book. Shortly afterward, Murasaki, and then Genji, pass from the scene, and the Karma of their lives is worked out in a narrative of profundity and insight not even to be approached until Marcel Proust.

AKAZOME EMON (?–1027) was the daughter of Taira no Kanemori, the poet and statesman, and the wife of Ōe no Masahira. She was Lady in Waiting to Rinko, the wife of the great minister (Kampaku) Michinaga. She is a later member of the great group of women poets, roughly contemporary with Murasaki and the author of the *Eiga-Monogatari,* the story of the supremacy of the Fujiwara, an unusual type of book for a Japanese woman to write at any time.

SEI SHŌNAGON lived in the 10th Century, a contemporary of Murasaki Shikibu. She was the daughter of Kiyowara no Motosuke and Lady of Honor to Teishi, the other consort of the Emperor Ichijō. Her *Pillow Book* (*Makura no Sōshi*) is one of the major works of Japanese literature, a seemingly random collection of notes and observations, characterized throughout by her rather waspish temper which is amusing enough in context but which vitiates her poems as poems. This poem is an echo of a very famous early anonymous poem in the *Kokinshū Anthology*.

> Yoshino River
> Flows between Imo Mountain
> And Mt. Se. All the
> World's illusion
> Flows between lover and lover.

Imo and Se, big brother and little sister, are terms of endearment between lovers and husband and wife. There are actually such hills above the Yoshino River. The original may well be an Utagaki, one of the songs sung in group courtship dances on opposite sides of running water.

MOTHER OF MICHITSUNA is known only by this name or as the wife of the regent Kaneie. She lived at the end of the 10th Century at the beginning of the great blossoming of women poets, some years earlier than Izumi Shikibu.

DAINI NO SANMI (10th–11th Century) was the daughter of Murasaki Shikibu, and is known by her rank of honor, the Third Sanmi, and the title of her father or husband, Daini. Women in the Heian Period were seldom known by personal names. It is not true that they did not have them, but the failure to use them is the survival of primitive taboos. To this day Japanese are a little shocked by Americans who call them by their first names as soon as they get to know them.

IZUMI SHIKIBU (11th Century) was the daughter of Ōe no Masamune, the Lord of Echizen, and the wife of Tachibana no Michisada, Lord of Izumi. (Shikibu is not a name but the title of an office.) Her daughter, Ko-Shikibu no Naishi, was also a poet. Izumi became Lady in Waiting to the Empress Ichijō. She separated from her husband and became the lover of Prince Tametaka and, after his death, of his brother Prince Atsumichi. There survives a book of her poetry and her diary, one of the masterpieces of Japanese literature. Most of her poetry is erotic: she seems to have spent a life largely devoted to making love. It is characterized by a dreamy eroticism full of Buddhist feeling of the impermanence of all things, most of all love. She seems to have led an interesting life.

ISE TAYŪ (11th Century) was the daughter of Ōnakatomi no Sukechika, the chief priest of the Ise Shrine.

LADY SAGAMI was Lady in Waiting to Princess Yūshi in the 11th Century and married Oe no Kinyori, Lord of Sagami, who divorced her when she became the lover of Fujiwara no Sadayori.

LADY SUWŌ was the daughter of Tsugunaka, Governor of Suwō, and a Lady in Waiting (Naishi) at the court of the Emperor Go-Reizei (1046–1069).

PRINCESS SHIKISHI (?–1201) was the daughter of the Emperor Go-Shirakawa. She became the princess of the Kamo Shrine in Kyoto, one of the principal shrines of Shintō. Later she became a Buddhist nun. She is one of the last of the great women poets of the Heian Court and lived on into the 13th Century.

KENREI MON-IN UKYO NO DAIBU (12th Century) was a Lady in Waiting to Kenrei Mon-in, the consort of the Emperor Takakura, the daughter of Taira no Kiyomori, who was overthrown by Minamoto no Yoritomo, and was involved in the tragic end of Taira power.

THE LADY GIŌ ("Girl of Art") is one of the heroines of the history-romance the *Heike Monogatari*. She was the mistress of Taira no Kiyomori (1118–1181). She and her sister Ginyo were daughters of the white dress dancer, Toji, the most famous of their time. After she had been the favorite of Kiyomori for three years, a sixteen-year-old girl called Hotoke, or Lady Buddha, arrived in the capital and became famous as a white dress dancer. She presented herself at the palace but was turned away by Kiyomori. Giō interceded for her, and she sang and danced and captivated the dictator, who then transferred his favors to her. She begged to be allowed to depart, but he would not permit it, and he expelled Giō from the palace. A year later Kiyomori demanded that she return to the palace and perform. He then insisted that she become a handmaiden of Hotoke. This humiliation drove Giō and her mother and her sister to the point of suicide, but they decided instead to become nuns. Early that autumn, during the night of the Tanabata Festival, there was a rapping at the door of their retreat. It was Hotoke who had come to join them as a nun. So perfect was their devotion that all four entered Nirvana. There is still a small temple with their statues in one of the most beautiful sites in Arashiyama, the western hills of Kyoto, famous for the splendor of its autumn leaves. It is the only temple in Japan dedicated to women who were not supernatural beings.

The poem was written on the sliding door of Giō's room as she left the palace the first time and was repeated by Hotoke as she entered the nun's retreat.

YOKOBUE lived in the 12th Century. Near the temple of Giō and the other women is a small shrine to Yokobue, heroine of another brief but poignant episode in the *Heike Monogatari*. She was a servant to Kenrei Mon-in. *Yokobue* means flute player. Tokiyori, the son of a courtier, fell in love with her but his father forbade him to have anything to do with her as he had already planned an influential marriage for his son. Tokiyori shaved his head and became a monk. When she heard this, Yokobue went seeking him and wandered toward Saga (not the modern town) above the Oi River. Under the full moon, in the time of plum blossoms, she heard the voice of Tokiyori chanting Sutras. Yokobue sent him a message but he turned her away and then went to the great Shingon Temple complex at Mt. Kōya. There he heard that she had become a nun. They exchanged poems and shortly afterward she died in Nara, but her shrine is in Arashiyama.

Takiguchi Nyūdo Tokiyori

I sorrowed in this world of sorrows
until I shaved my head.
Now I have learned
that you have become a nun
in bliss we shall go the same Way,
two arrows shot from a catalpa wood
   bow,
never to return.

SHIZUKA (12th Century) was a white dress dancer of spectacular beauty who became the lover of Minamoto no Yoshitsune, the tragic hero of the epic of the war between the Taira and Minamoto which brought to an end the great years of early Japanese civilization. He was the principal general of his brother Yoritomo, and broke the power of the Taira in a series of battles. When Yoritomo and his courtiers were worshipping at the Tsuruga-Oka Shrine at Kamakura, he commanded Shizuka to perform her most famous dance. She refused but was finally forced. She danced, singing two songs, of which we give one. Shortly after, she gave birth to Yoshitsune's son, whom Yoritomo murdered. She then became a Buddhist nun and lived to an old age long after Yoshitsune had been destroyed in his refuge in the far North. She is not a great poet but, with Yoshitsune, one of the great tragic figures of Japanese history. Her dance occurs in several Noh plays.

LADY HORIKAWA was an attendant on Dowager Empress Taiken in the 12th Century.

THE DAUGHTER OF MINAMOTO NO TOSHITAKA (12th Century) is known in the *Hyakunin-Isshu* as Kōka Monin no Bettō, which means the High Stewardess of the Dowager Empress Kōka. This poem is famous among English translators for its organization of puns which make it two quite different poems:

> For the sake of one node
> of a reed of Naniwa bay,
> must I wade out
> past the depth measuring gauge?

With a little manipulation of *Kanji,* Chinese characters, and *Kana,* Japanese syllabary, it would be possible to get still a third poem out of it. Naniwa is modern Ōsaka.

SHUNZEI'S DAUGHTER (1171–1252) is known by no other name. She was the sister of the great poet Sada-ie, known as Teika. Her father, her brother, Toshiyori, Toshimoto, and Saigyō the monk, were leaders of a revolution of the sensibility in the late 12th Century and first half of the 13th Century. Shunzei is also known by the name he took when he became a Buddhist monk, Shaku-a. In those days there began a long period of civil wars that brought Heian civilization to an end.

ABUTSU-NI was Maid of Honor to the Princess Kuni-Naishinnō and then the wife of Fujiwara Tameie, the son of the great poet Sadaie, who was the son of the equally great poet Toshinari, called Teika. She was thus part of the late 12th and early 13th Century revolution of the sensibilities, the last great moment of classical Japanese poetry. In 1277 she went from Kyōto to Kamakura for a lawsuit regarding the inheritance for herself and Tameie's sons and wrote a diary of her journey, the *Izayoi Nikki,* one of the classics of Japanese prose.

HAIKU POETS OF THE TOKUGAWA PERIOD

KAWAI CHIGETSU-NI (1632–1736) was born in Ōtsu on Lake Ōmi. She was the pupil of Bashō and the mother of the poet Otokuni.

DEN SUTE-JO (1633–1698) was the wife of a judge in Tamba Province. After her husband's death she became a nun. She is most famous for her "Snowy Morning" poem, written at the age of six.

ŌME SHUSHIKI (1668–1725) was the wife of Kangyoku, a teacher of *haiku* in Edo (Tokyo) and the pupil of Kikaku, Bashō's favorite disciple. Her famous poem was written at the age of thirteen during the cherry viewing festival in Ueno Park in Tokyo. Today on cherry viewing Sunday in Ueno the park is literally packed with people, a large percentage of them full of sake. The next morning the park, the largest in Tokyo, is literally knee-deep in picnic litter. A sprout of Shushiki's tree still stands by the well with a plaque bearing the poem.

CHINE-JO (Late 17th Century) was a sister of Kyorai, one of the ten great disciples of Bashō.

FUKUDA CHIYO-NI (1703–1775) was born in Matsutō, the wife of a samurai servant. Her husband died when she was twenty-seven and the next year her only son died. She became a nun and studied with the *haiku* teachers Shikō and Rogembō. She is considered the greatest woman writer of *haiku*. The *haiku* on the death of her son has been translated into many languages. She was also a painter.

UKIHASHI (Late 17th Century) was a courtesan of the type of cultivated entertainers who would later become *geisha*. This haiku is popularly believed to be that of Chiyo-Ni, but it is actually Ukihashi's.

ENOMOTO SEIFU-JO (1731–1814) was a student of the *haiku* poet Shiro of the school of Issa.

MATSUMOTO KOYŪ-NI (Late 18th Century)

IMAIZUMI SOGETSU-NI (?–1804) was the wife of Tsunenaru, a teacher of *haiku*.

TAGAMI KIKUSHA-NI (1752–1826)

MODERN TANKA POETS

YOSANO AKIKO (1878–1942) was the daughter of Ōtori, a merchant in the ancient trading city of Sakai, now absorbed into the Ōsaka metropolitan area. She graduated from Sakai Girls' High School and in 1900 went to Tōkyō, studied poetry with Yosano Hiroshi (Tekkan), who considered himself the leader of the new *waka* poetry *(tanka)* movement, and soon married him. For a while, in Tōkyō and Kyōto they were involved in a tragic *maison a trois* with a young woman, Yamakawa Tomiko, whom they both loved deeply. After a few years Tomiko died of tuberculosis. Akiko and Hiroshi founded the "New Poetry Society" and its organ, the magazine *Myōjō*, "Morning Star." Hiroshi always thought of himself as the genius of the family, although he was a sentimental and commonplace poet who learned little from the French Symbolists whom he adored. Akiko was quickly recognized and earned enough money to send Hiroshi to Paris from 1911 to 1914, but she was only able to save enough money for herself to stay part of 1912, and members of her family assisted them both to return to Japan. She wrote many collections of poetry, novels, essays, children's stories, and fairy tales. She did a complete translation, of great beauty of style, of *The Tale of Genji* into modern Japanese. But the day before the manuscript was to go to the publisher, the great Tokyo earthquake of 1923 struck and all copies were destroyed. She bravely set to work and did it all over within the year. She was a leading feminist and pacifist and socialist sympathizer. Her poem against the Russo-Japanese War was the first direct criticism of the Emperor ever printed except in political pamphlets, and she wrote in defense and in memorial of the socialist and anarchist martyrs of 1912 whose execution shocked the world—much as the executions of the Haymarket Martyrs and Sacco and Vanzetti did.

She is the only truly great poet to write in traditional *tanka* form in modern times. She and Hiroshi thought of themselves as stylistic revolutionaries, but in fact her poems are full of echoes of the classics and some are deliberately modeled on well known *Manyōshū* poems. But then, behind every renaissance of poetry in *tanka* form in Japan has lain a return to the purity of the *Manyō*. Akiko is more than this. She is one of the world's greatest women poets, comparable to Christina Rossetti, Gaspara Stampa, Louise Labe, and Li Ch'ing Chao. She is certainly one of the very greatest poets of her time—the most perfect expression of the "Art Nouveau" sensibility—like Debussy, who should have set her poems to music.

She lived until 1942, productive to the end, having betimes in her literary career also mothered eleven children.

YAMAKAWA TOMIKO (1879–1909) was born in a small village now part of Kohama, Fukui Prefecture, and graduated from Girls' High School in Osaka, which seems to have been one of the best secondary schools for women in its day. She studied for a year at Women's University in Tokyo, and married at twenty-one. Her husband died a few years later and she herself died at thirty, leaving one book, *Koi-Goromo (The Garment of Lovemaking)*, written in collaboration with Yosano Akiko and Chino Masako. She and Akiko were both lovers of Yosano Tekkan and of each other. She is the "lily" of Akiko's and Tekkan's poems and Akiko is the "white lespedeza" and Takino, Tekkan's first wife, is "white hibiscus." The relations of these three women and Chino Masako with each other and with Tekkan were extraordinarily complex and intense. Tekkan was a typical emotional exploiter of women. He attempted to disguise these proclivities with romantic nonsense about the spiritual glories of clandestine polygamy. Tomiko attempted to escape by marrying, but her husband died within two years, when she was twenty-three. When she was twenty-eight and being treated for tuberculosis at Kyōto University Hospital, she received word that her father was dying of tuberculosis. She tried to return to her native village but the snowfall was too deep. Eventually a family servant carried her on his back, wading through the snow. She went to bed immediately on her arrival and her father died shortly thereafter. Tomiko followed him in the spring. The poems which resulted from this tragic relationship of the women manipulated by a mediocre and emotionally crooked man are among their most moving. Many cannot be understood without reference to their "flower names" and to various other personal code terms. However, to this day there are still Japanese men who will inform you that Tekkan was a great poet and Akiko just a money-writer. The poem "I leave all the scarlet flowers" is probably Tomiko's death poem.

CHINO MASAKO (1880–1946) was born in Ōsaka, graduated from Women's University in Tokyo, and was married to Chino Shōshō, a poet and professor of German. She visited Europe and became a professor at Women's University.

KUJŌ TAKEKO (1877–1928) was a daughter of the Abbot of the West Honganji Temple in Kyōto. At twenty-two she married Baron Yoshimasa Kūjo and left with him for Europe. After a year and a half she returned alone to Japan and lived a solitary life until her diplomat husband returned. Most of her best poems are on loneliness. In spite of her submissive faithfulness to her husband, or perhaps because of it, she was an active leader of various socially concerned women's organizations of the Shinshū sect. As in America, such activities were the most effective outlet for the incipient feminism of the 19th Century. Her poems, with which most lonely Japanese wives could identify, were immensely popular.

OKAMOTO KANOKO (1889–1939) was born in Tokyo, studied at Sakurai English School, and was married to Okamoto Ippei, a famous caricaturist. She published novels, plays, and several collections of poetry.

GOTŌ MIYOKO (1898–) was born in Tokyo and studied *tanka* under Sasaki Nobutsuna. She published works in the magazine "Kokoro no Hana" (The Heart's Flower) and founded "Nyonin Tanka" (Women's

Tanka). Her book *Haha no Kashū (Tanka for Mother)* won the Yomiuri Literature Prize in 1957. Her poems on her dead daughter are among her best. She traveled in Europe and taught Japanese literature at Senshū-daigaku College.

HATSUI SHIZUE (1900–) was born in Hyōgo Prefecture and studied with Kitahara Hakushū, a leading poet of the first quarter of the 20th Century. She is one of the founders of "Nyonin Tanka" and "Cosmos," and the editor of a *tanka* column for the Yomiuri newspaper. Her many books of *tanka* have won several prizes.

ANRYŪ SUHARU (1923–) was born in Kyoto and worked for many years as a dressmaker. However, she has been ill and bedridden for several years. She is a *tanka* poet of the Tama group under the leadership of Miya Shūji.

BABA AKIKO (1928–) was born in Tokyo and graduated from Shōwa Women's University. She is a scholar with a profound understanding of classical *tanka* and *yōkyoku*, the lyrics of the classical Noh drama. She is not only one of the best contemporary writers of *tanka* but has written extensively on classical Japanese literature, from the beginning to the Tokugawa Shōgunate. Her representative collection of *tanka* is *Mugen Kajo*.

MODERN HAIKU POETS

SUGITA HISAJO (1890–1946) was born in Kagoshima, the southernmost city of the main islands of Japan. She married a high school teacher of painting with whom she does not seem to have lived a very happy life. She was a passionate woman who managed to compress an intense erotic sensibility similar to the great Heian women of the *Kokinshū* like Izumi and Komachi into brief *haiku*. She became a leader among the women *haiku* poets of the group *Hototogisu* (The Cuckoo) and founded her own magazine *Hanagoromo* (The Flowered Kimono). She was dismissed from her school for her eccentricity, and later became insane and died in a hospital.

MITSUHASHI TAKAJO (1899–1972) began as a disciple of Yosano Akiko but as a *haiku* rather than a *tanka* poet. She lived a life of remarkable asceticism and spiritual concentration and came to write poems of total self-alienation of the vanishing of the empiric ego in the Void, although her Void resembles Kierkegaard's rather than the Buddhist concept.

HASHIMOTO TAKAKO (1899–1963) is a *haiku* poet who resembles one of the lesser American Objectivists.

NAKAMURA TEIJO (1900–   ) was born in Kumamoto and is a representative poet of the *Hototogisu* School who writes mostly of her domestic life.

HOSHINO TATSUKO (1903–)is the daughter of the leader of the *Hototogisu* School, Takahama Kyoshi. Like the other women of the group, her poems deal with domestic life and the happiness of ordinary living.

YAGI MIKAJO (1924–   ) was born in Ōsaka and studied with Hirahata Seito, a *haiku* poet and psychiatrist, and became an ophthamologist. She writes typical modern haiku.

FREE VERSE POETS

YOSANO AKIKO (1878–1942)

FUKAO SUMAKO (1893–1974) was born into an old family in Hyōgo Prefecture which became impoverished after the death of her father. Her husband died when she was still young and she became a friend of Yosano Akiko (whose biography she was later to write) and was strongly influenced by her poetry, her feminism, and her radical social ideas. She was one of the first Japanese poets to experience the alienation and revolution of the sensibilities that had become characteristic of the best Western poetry since Baudelaire, Holderlin, and Blake, apparently largely on her own at first, although she later traveled in Europe where she came under the influence of Colette. Her books shift gradually from purely personal revolt to concern with social issues and the psychological interactions of other human beings. After the Pacific War she went abroad again. Her last trip was through the Mideast, Eastern Europe, and China. Like all the sensitive people of her generation, she was deeply wounded by the devastation of Japan and its rule as a colony by the United States. Her later poems give expression to her sorrow, dismay, and resistance not only to the conquerers but to the later pollution and demoralization of Japan's runaway booming new capitalism.

HAYASHI FUMIKO (1904–1951) was taken by her mother from her father when she was eight years old and spent the rest of her childhood wandering over Japan with her mother's second husband, a peddler. Homeless and often hungry, she went to work early and held a wide variety of poor working class jobs. Her themes are the hard life of the poorest working-class women and their brutalization by their men. She is more than simply a Naturalist writer. Her poetry communicates the most intense feelings of reality voiced with presentational immediacy.

NAGASE KIYOKO (1906–) was born in Okayama Prefecture. Her poems of a woman's life express a profound sense of the unity of all human beings.

NAKAMURA CHIO (1913–) was an early contributor to Kitazono Katsue's magazine of Esprit Nouveau, VOU, the leading publication of international "Modernist" poetry between the wars. ("VOU" is not Japanese. Kitasono says it means "vow.") With Fukao Sumako she established the Association of Japanese Women Poets and published an anthology of their work. "A Diary

Without Dates" is the title poem of her third book of verse, written on the death of her husband.

TAKADA TOSHIKO (1916–   ) ran a weekly column open to modern poetry in Asahi, Japan's largest newspaper. The column and her own poems are very popular with Japanese women. (Almost all Japanese newspapers publish a great deal of poetry.)

TAKIGUCHI MASAKO (1933–   ) was born in Seoul where she lost everything during the Pacific War and was returned to Japan. On the whole her poems are better written than those of most social poets, but they are also full of personal bitterness. Her feminist poems are violently cynical. In "At the Slaughterhouse," a woman's body in sexual intercourse and the body of a cow being slaughtered are overlapped. She received the Murō Saisei Prize for her books *Aoi Uma (Blue Horses)* and *Kōtetsu no Ashi (Legs of Steel)*. She works as a librarian at the National Diet Library.

MITSUI FUTABAKO (1919–   ) at first wrote poetry influenced by her father Saijō Yaso, a leading Symbolist. She later turned to a more contemporary international idiom. Her poems express the pain, anxiety, and alienation of a person of sensitivity caught in the destruction of values in our collapsing world civilization. However, she writes with a dry brilliance and sense of balance. Characteristically, she translated Supervielle.

ISHIGAKI RIN (1920–   ) is probably the leading woman poet of social protest. Unmarried, she supported her sick father and stepmother as an office worker in a Tōkyō bank for forty years, a situation she met with merciless realism. Few poets have written so well of the monotony of poorly-paid women office laborers. Unlike many much younger women to whom "women's lib" (a term not used by feminists in America) is just the latest U.S. fad, she is aware that the subjugation of women is far more a social question than a sexual one. Like the great novelist Kobayashi, author of *The Cannery Boat,* and B. Traven, she is one of the few genuinely proletarian writers. Perhaps because her problems are real rather than psychological, she writes with considerable dry humor.

SHINDŌ CHIE (1920–) studied at the Athenée Francaise in Tokyo and was influenced by French Symbolism, and later by more modern French poets.

IBARAGI NORIKO (1926–) was born in Ōsaka and is one of the strongest social poets of the present time. Much of her poetry is concerned with aspects of the economic and political crises of the final phase of world capitalism. But even her domestic poetry, possibly because of her revolutionary philosophy, has an unusual toughness. She is one of the most active and best-known Japanese women poets and might be compared to Muriel Rukeyser and Denise Levertov in the United States.

FUKUNAKA TOMOKO (1928–) has been much influenced by Japanese popular songs and American pseudo-folk songs. She hosts a radio program, "Rainbow Fantasy," on an Osaka FM station. She might be best compared to the American Rod McKuen.

FUKUI HISAKO (1929–) was born in Kōbe. She teaches at Kōbe Yamate Women's College and has published several books of poems including *Kudamono to Naifu (Fruit and Knife)* (1958), *Umi Kujira no Tōru Michi (The Sea, the Path Where Whales Pass)* (1969), and *Tori to Aoi Toki (Bird and Blue Time)*. Some of her poems are written from the point of view of her child.

SHINKAWA KAZUE (1929–) studied with Saijō Yaso, a leader of Japanese Symbolism (which differs considerably from French Symbolism). Like many now-forgotten American women poets of the early Twenties, she writes of what used to be called "free love." She has won a Murō Saisei Prize.

INOUE MICHIKO (?–?) is a poet of the VOU group, along with Shiraishi Kazuko and Nakamura Chio. She might be considered a predecessor of the fully developed poetry of Shiraishi.

TADA CHIMAKO (1930–) is more learned and more philosophical in the Western sense than most Japanese poets. (Except for professors of the subject, most Japanese intellectuals consider "Dekahe" (Descartes, Kant, Hegel), and what passes for profound philosophy in the West, to be simply a peculiar form of bad manners.) Tada Chimako, however, is genuinely profound by either Eastern or Western standards. She has been influenced by Greek, Hellenistic, and Byzantine, as well as by contemporary French literature. Her poems are a kind of epitaph on the movement of her thoughts on time and herself. She has translated, from the French, authors as dissimilar as St. Jean Perse and Levi-Strauss. Recently she has become interested in Buddhism. Her home is in Kōbe.

SHIRAISHI KAZUKO (1931–) was born in Vancouver and came to Japan when she was seven years old. She was first published in Kitazono Katsue's magazine VOU as a young girl and later developed a personal style related to the Angry Young Men in England, the Beats in America, and Voznesensky in Russia, although her most direct influence was Dylan Thomas. With Tomioka Taeko and Kenneth Rexroth she introduced poetry and jazz to Japan at the Pit Inn in 1967. She continued her readings through the years when the medium went out of fashion around the world, so today she is a leader in the revival at least as impressive as the French chanteuse Brigitte Fontaine or any American. In recent years she has been writing long poems which speak out of the chaos and horror of modern civilization of a vision of a kind of cosmic sexuality. She has published many books, won many prizes, writes magazine columns and prose fiction, and frequently appears on television. She is probably Japan's leading contemporary poet, male or female, and is immensely popular with young women. Her eminence is recognized even by the most respectable men critics, and most Japanese poets would readily agree that she is the second greatest poet in the country, themselves of course being first. She is far more a traditional writer than the American Japanologist who dismissed her with what he thought was an insult, "the Japanese Allen Ginsberg," seems to be aware. She writes in the tradition which stretches in modern times from the 17th Century writer of the loves and sorrows of *geisha* and prostitutes and the greed and brutality of newly rich merchants, Ihara Saikaku, to the 20th Century novelist of the dying pleasure quarters and the cheap cafe theaters and the love-lost prostitutes and their customers of the slums, Nagai Kafū.

YOSHIHARA SACHIKO (1932–) was born in Tokyo and graduated from Tokyo University, majoring in French. In her first two books of poems she sought to recapture the innocence and immediacy of response of childhood. She has come to write more and more on the love of women. Trained as an actress, she is a popular and extraordinarily effective reader of her own poetry. "Blasphemy" and "I Forget" are translated by John Solt and Nakagawa Kazuyo.

KŌRA RUMIKO (1932–) has written both prose and poetry expressing the widespread opposition to the Japan-U.S.A. Security Treaty and the influence of American imperialism on Japanese economics and politics as well as in opposition to the Vietnam War. These are not, however, her exclusive subjects. Her poetry has been deeply influenced by Francis Ponge and the French Structuralists and by American Objectivism. She played an active role in the Asia-Africa Writer's Conference in 1970 and in similar activities since that time.

TOMIOKA TAEKO (1935–) was born in Ōsaka and graduated from Ōsaka Women's College. After graduation she moved to Tokyo and married. She has translated Gertrude Stein's work and her poems show the influence of Stein and the French poets of the Cubist generation. Although her poems are very radical in syntax, they are deeply rooted in Japanese tradition. Like so many of Japan's leading modernists of the generation just before her, she writes of the demoralization of Japanese society by Japan's own peculiar "post-modern" development, so often wrongly called Westernization, and especially of the effects on women of this culture clash. In recent years she has turned to writing fiction and has become one of the best-known Japanese novelists.

YOSHIYUKI RIE (1939–) was born in Tokyo and graduated from Waseda University. Her poetry is sensual and visionary. Recently she has turned from writing poetry to fiction.

ATSUMI IKUKO (1940–) was born in Central Japan to a family of scholars, and now teaches American literature at Aoyama Gakuin, one of the largest universities in Japan. She contributes poetry to the poetry magazines of Japan and English-speaking countries and is also an influential critic. She has edited the letters and written a biography of Yone Noguchi. Her own poems have been gathered in a *Collected Poems of Atsumi Ikuko*. She has just completed a volume of criticism on the women poets of America and has collaborated with others in the translation of modern Japanese poetry into English. She is a dedicated feminist—a movement that is growing in popularity in Japan as fast as it is in the United States. Ms. Atsumi has traveled through the United States and Canada and was a guest at the Iowa International Writer's Workshop, and has lectured extensively in both countries, in both languages.

KANAI MIEKO (1947–) is a poet and novelist of eroticism and violence who came out of the revolt of youth of the late Sixties. Her poetry combines influences of modern French literature and popular Japanese culture. She has also written several novels.

NISHI JUNKO (?–) disappeared leaving two small mimeographed collections of her poems, *Nagai Tegami (Long Letters)* and *Monogatari (Story)*, published in Amagasaki, Hyōgo Prefecture, in 1970.

THE GEISHA SONGS are all anonymous and date from at least before the First World War. The last four are simplifications of famous classic Japanese poems which appear in Rexroth's *100 Poems From the Japanese* or *100 More Poems From the Japanese* or in this book. All are in the twenty-six syllable form called *dodoitsu*. Most modern day *geisha* know these songs and can sing them on demand. "Modern geisha," that is, *geisha* who wear modern dress and do not behave in the traditional manner, of course sing modern songs.

II.
The Women Poets of Japan—A Brief Survey

The current prominence of women poets in Japanese literature is not new. There have been two periods in the country's long literary history from the 7th Century to the present when women poets flourished. The first was in the time of the earliest writers in the *Manyō-shū (The Collection of 10,000 Leaves)*, compiled in the latter half of the 8th Century but containing many examples of older poetry. The second was in Heian times when the capital had been established permanently in Kyōto in the 8th Century. This period lasted until the break-up of Heian culture in the civil wars which came to an end with the subjection of the Emperor and court in Kyōto to the Tokugawa Shōguns, who then moved the capital to Edo, the modern Tokyo. There are two historical works, the *Kojiki* and the *Nihon Shoki*, the first part of each of which is mythical, in which occur poems reputedly written, or rather uttered, by women. However, since these works were in fact written down after the compilation of the *Manyōshū* there is no way of knowing which of these songs and poems uttered by goddesses and early royalty were in fact the work of women.

Most of the poems in these two books and the so-called long poems of the *Manyōshū* (which are not long by Western standards) do show that Japanese poetry had tended from the earliest times to use a prosody of alternating or sometimes varied lines of five and seven syllables. By the time the capital had been settled in Nara, the first poems in the *Manyōshū* had been collected. The *waka* of thirty-one syllables arranged five, seven, five, seven, seven, had become the common form and even the Naga Uta long poems usually concluded with a kind of coda in *waka* form. A few poems were *sedōka*, arranged five-seven-seven-five-seven-seven, thirty-eight syllables. The Naga Uta and the *sedōka* were soon abandoned. Exclusive of poems in Chinese and folk songs, the latter being almost always in lines of five and seven syllables as in the common *dodoitsu*, arranged seven-seven-five, containing twenty-six syllables, the *tanka* or *waka* became the only form to be used until the development of the *haiku* of only seventeen syllables in the Edo period.

The *Manyōshū* was written in an extraordinary use of Chinese characters. Sometimes the character meant what it said. More often, the character represented the archaic Japanese pronunciation of the Chinese ideogram. There are many passages in the *Manyōshū* whose meaning is the subject of controversy to this day. In spite of the difficulty of the script, a little more than one-third of the *Manyōshū* poets can be recognized as women, excluding anonymous authors who wrote as females. The script known as Manyōgana was probably employed largely as a mnemonic and the poems were transmitted orally, usually sung or chanted, as they still are to this day. Certainly in later centuries very few women learned to write Chinese characters. Whoever may have edited the *Manyōshū*, the canon was closed before the capital moved to Kyoto, with 4,516 poems in all. The standard English translation contains 1,000 poems.

The remarkable thing about the *Manyōshū* is its extraordinary democracy. There are poems by emperors and empresses, princes and princesses, generals and lonely common soldiers on the then-narrow frontiers of Japan, beggars, monks, and courtesans. A whole section was devoted to "Eastland Poems," probably in a different dialect from an area which was in those days the Eastern border of Imperial Japan and is still relatively backward country today.

Toward the end of the 8th Century two syllabaries of fifty characters each were developed. Their invention is attributed to Kōbō-daishi or Kūkai (7 7 4—8 3 5), who introduced Shingon or esoteric Buddhism to Japan, and are usually considered to have been developed from far more complicated Chinese characters of the same pronunciation. Some scholars have pointed out that all sorts of things dating from those times are attributed to Kōbō-daishi: bridges, roads, temples, and so forth. They have also noted that many Kana letters resemble the peculiar distortions of Sanskrit writing used by Japanese monks. Hiragana was also called *onna-de* (women's writing). Katakana was an angular script which does not blend well with either Hiragana or Kanji, and which is commonly used for transliterating foreign words, for children's books, and telegrams. Although there are fifty principle characters in each syllabary, there are altogether one hundred twelve symbols in each. The additional ones modify by short strokes like quotation marks, a circle, or a diminutive of the symbols for the syllables *yu, ya,* and *yo.* All the symbols except one final nasal (usually *n* but sometimes *m*) represent syllables ending in vowels. In the classical period, in the recitation of classical poetry, and in some contemporary dialects, the final nasal is vocalized as *nu* or *mu.*

The invention of Hiragana opened Japanese literature to women. The great age of women writers, which took place after the capital had been established at Kyōto and was certainly the greatest period of women writers in the history of any literature, owed much to Hiragana. It should not be forgotten however that Japanese is full of homonyms, and anything written exclusively in the syllabary or in the Western alphabet, known as rōmaji, would often lapse into incomprehensibility if the ambiguous sound was not represented by a Chinese character. So it is not quite true that the great women writers of the Heian Period were totally ignorant of Chinese, although very few poems written by women exclusively in Chinese survive from those days. Murasaki Shikibu and Sei Shōnagon are among the few exceptions.

Men wrote mostly in Chinese characters and in careful imitation of Chinese models, not in *waka.* For a couple of centuries it has been fashionable to deprecate these poems. In fact, many of them are quite beautiful, although none are very original as they directly echo the themes and devices of Chinese poetry, usually of the

Six Dynasties Period or of the T'ang poet Po Chu-i. Although this close imitation of classical models in a foreign language robs most poetry of emotional spontaneity, this is not always true. No one echoes Greek forms and themes more than Catullus, the most passionate of all Roman poets, but if a Japanese Catullus exists he is not well known to Japanologists. So the expression of spontaneous emotion, exquisite sensibility, and love was left largely to women.

In the early Heian Period, a lingering social memory survived from the days when the Yamato invaders of central Honshu, the main island, were often ruled by queens who were also shamanesses, and when the family economic structure and clan relationships were dominated by women. In fact, Japan, which many foreigners unfamiliar with the real life of the country consider a land of happily submissive women, was in its beginnings probably the nearest thing to that matriarchy sought so fervently at the beginnings of history throughout the world. There may never have been any Amazons in Anatolia but there were certainly powerful empresses in Japan at the dawn of history, and the Empress Jingū, the conquerer of Korea in the 3rd or 4th Century, was certainly a real person. Incidentally, she seems to have governed by receiving revelations on national policy much as the founders of the Quakers, the Mormons, and the Shakers did. Most importantly, many of the so-called "New Religions" of Japan are still governed this way.

In Japan, even more than in China, poetry assumed a ceremonial importance in the life of the court, and highly formal court parties were often largely given over to what we would call "poetry contests." It should be borne in mind that at such times the poems were chanted or even sung rather than recited in an ordinary voice, and to this day there are famous poetry chanters of *waka* whose patterns are somewhat similar to those of Gregorian chants. Besides their ceremonial use, *waka* also played a far more intimate, personal role than poetry did in China.

The novels and diaries of the Heian Period are full of

poems, and the accepted form of courtship was an exchange of poems which usually masked their erotic meaning under nature symbolism. Even as late as the *Tale of Genji,* courtship bears a certain resemblance to the practices of some South Seas peoples. The man may never have seen the woman but has fallen in love with the beautiful arrangement of the overlapping sleeves of her many kimono, which were carefully allowed to hang over the side of her ox-cart when she was on pilgrimage. Poems would be presented tied to a spray of wild plum or red maple leaves or willow catkins, depending on the season and, incidentally, were expected to contain key words that identified them with the season. No matter how much the woman may have wished to discourage her suitor, it was unforgivable to not answer.

Because a woman of the court was sheltered behind sliding walls and papered screens and then behind a portable screen draped with cloth—and days or weeks might pass before the enamored courtier caught a glimpse of her—the poems passed back and forth through servants. Ivan Morris says that the aristocratic women of those days lived in semi-darkness, but the inner court of the women's apartments, which usually contained its own garden, was open to the light, and the women's rooms were fairly well lit at night. However, even when the lover penetrated all the defenses of screens and maids he seldom saw very much of his beloved. There is no mention in classical Japanese literature of even semi-nudity in lovemaking, and the much later *Shunga,* erotic color prints, are largely displays of elaborate fabrics which reveal only the faces and the exaggerated sexual organs of the lovers. Early Japanese architecture, as it survives in the great Shintō Shrines, has often been compared with that of the South Seas, but Japanese lovemaking, at least as the classic novels and diaries pretend it was practiced, bears an even more striking resemblance to the "creep courtship" of the South Seas.

It is not enough to read Japanese *waka* in the Imperial anthologies. It must be understood in the context of ceremonial court functions, poetry contests, and the highly specialized upper-class love making. Success in love depended much on the exquisiteness of the sensibility displayed, in the choice of words of the *waka,* and on the even more exquisite aesthetics of the calligraphy.

All this applies to the poetry which begins with the first Imperial anthology, the *Kokinshū.* Things appear to have been much freer and less highly formalized in the Asuka and Nara days when the *Manyōshū* was gathered. Men and women circulated freely together and there is some indication that women even accompanied men on the great hunts of still half-wild Japan, and also appeared publicly at court functions and parties. The love poetry of the *Manyōshū* is far more typical of the Western point of view than that of later ages in Japanese literature.

Quite a few love poems between princes and princesses are collected in the early part of the *Manyōshū.* Princess Nukada, one of the finest poets in the first part of the *Manyōshū,* lived in the turbulent time of the establishment of the Imperial Clan as the rulers of Japan. She, like Sappho, is half-legendary, but is considered to have been a divine messenger, an oracle or shamaness, and a public poet. Her greatness lies in her ability to combine in universal terms the expression of personal passion and powerful collective emotion—and in the extraordinary beauty of her sonorous poetry, which would seem to show a long period of conscious aesthetic development from the pre-literate poetry gathered in the *Kojiki* and the *Nihon Shoki.*

Representative of the second period is Yosami, one of the wives of Hitomaro who is usually considered Japan's greatest poet. Yosami's poems of marital love share with Hitomaro's the same sense of intimate comradeship and freedom of movement so unlike the formularized behavior of the ladies in the *Tale of Genji.*

The leading woman poet of the third period of the *Manyōshū* is Sakanoe no Iratsume. Although she was married several times and had two children, she was forced to assume control of her family, the Ōtomo. The family was under persistent attack from the leading court faction and would eventually, long after her death, be exterminated or driven into exile.

Kasa no Iratsume, in the last period of the *Manyō-shū*, was a lover of the great poet Ōtomo no Yakamo-chi. She used a much freer vocabulary than the court poets who had preceded her and wrote with a new objectivity, or rather with a new objective expression of intensely personal subjectivity. In her poems things form a mold for love—"Last night I dreamed/I held a sword against my naked body./What does it mean?/It means I shall see you soon." This erotic intensity and tragic view of life (the Ōtomo family was already on the eve of extinction) linked her poems to the vertiginous eroticism of the great Heian women Izumi Shikubu and Ono no Komachi.

Inserted in the *Manyōshū* is an anthology of poems from eastern Japan, in those days as far east as the present Kanto Basin, where Tokyo now lies. One-third of the Eastland poems are by women. They show a greater influence of folk poetry, the short songs, or the long narrative ballads, the free relations of the frontier, and the sorrows of wives forced to live apart from their husbands—quite unlike the traditional lonely wife or abandoned concubine poems of Chinese literature which were usually written by men.

A peculiarity of the *Manyōshū* is the almost complete lack of poems showing any influence of Buddhism. In fact, there is only one poem which is specifically, overtly Buddhist. "I loathe the twin seas/Of being and not being/And long for the mountain/Of bliss untouched by/The changing tides." The poet is anonymous, but the poem's language indicates it may well have been written by a woman.

Two hundred years after the compilation of the *Manyōshū*, a group of leading poets of the court was ordered by the Emperor to compile the first of the Imperial Anthologies, the *Kokinshū*, or collection of ancient and modern Japanese poems. The poets were Ōshi-kōchi no Mitsune, Mibu no Tadamine, Ki no Tomo-nori, and others, under the general editorship of Ki no Tsurayuki (c. 868–946). Although most of them were not courtiers of the highest rank, they were considered the leading poets of their day. Tsurayuki's preface to the *Kokinshū*, which opens with the statement, "The poetry of Japan has its roots in the human heart and flourishes in countless leaves of words," is considered a masterpiece of classical Japanese (*kana*) prose and established the critical idiom for the judgment of poetry for generations.

In the *Kokinshū* there are twenty-eight women and one-hundred-twenty-two men or anonymous poets. The difference from the *Manyōshū* is pronounced. Gone is the old democracy. Almost all the poets are connected with the court or at least come from families of the highest aristocracy. The capital had moved to Kyoto and the court had assumed a rigid hierarchy patterned on the Chinese. The court, however, was not recruited by examinations open to the general upper class populace but determined by aristocracy of birth. The peculiar cloistering of women described earlier, with its attendant special mechanisms of courtship, had become established. It was a unique combination of purdah and promiscuity whose whole technique of interpersonal relations would have lead to the summary decapitation of practically all the characters in the *Tale of Genji* had it occurred in the Chinese court.

Although there are four times the number of men than women in the *Kokinshū*, the women are quite the equal of the men in acuteness of sensibility and, once the poems are decoded, in erotic interests. However, since polygamy was common, adolescent girls spent their time in lonely claustration learning to write *waka* in beautiful calligraphy to facilitate their opportunity for marriage. After marriage, even as today, the husband was quite likely to seek his erotic pleasures outside the home. This left his lonely wife behind her screens until, by lucky chance, the maid one morning presented her with a carefully inscribed *waka* on a beautifully folded piece of paper attached to a branch of flowering plum or spray of bush clover. Then might begin a long courtship of poetic interchange, culminating in first-night poems comparable to the bread-and-butter notes we send a hostess.

To understand the poetry of Japan from the *Kokinshū*, through all the Imperial anthologies, to the establishment of the pseudo-Confucianism of the Tokugawa Shōgunate, it is almost necessary to read the *Tale of Genji* and Ivan Morris' commentary on it, *The World of the Shining Prince*. It is curious that this strange combination of cloister and promiscuity with all its elaborate courtesies, its incredibly refined aestheticism, and its poignant abandoned eroticism, all of which are truly Japanese, has left little mark on the interpersonal culture of contemporary Japan. This is true even among the archaizers like Mishima or, in television and cinema, Sawano Hisao. Only Kawabata Yasunari deliberately modeled his work on Heian literature. The strangeness of this epoch to modern Japanese is shown by the general Japanese critical opinion that Kawabata's novels are influenced by the Tokugawa bourgeois *haiku*. One may note that all his novels are woman-centered as, behind the cliches of the "subjugation of women," was Heian court society. The men were warriors, high bureaucrats, governors, and administrators, but in the literature they seem to do nothing but slip under curtains, poems first, and then themselves.

Unlike the *Manyōshū*, the *Kokinshū* is saturated with the special aesthetics of Buddhism, *mono no aware*, the response of a refined sensibility to the pathos of the ephemeral beauty of the passing world. The poetry of the classical anthologies is usually arranged by season, and in each *waka* there is supposed to be at least one reference which sets the poem in time. This is a commonly applied rule of Chinese verse, beginning with the Six Dynasties, but in Japanese the seasonal reference always implies the fleeting world, "*yo no naka no.*"

Two of the greatest women poets of this time, the 9th Century, are Ono no Komachi and Lady Ise. Komachi's poems have a fierce, supple eroticism, while Lady Ise's are more intellectual. Komachi's legendary biography is derived from her poems and is embodied in three great Noh plays. Unlike the poetry of the *Manyōshū*, her poems are full of double meanings and contain words which, if divided into different words, enormously increase their complexity. This gives her work a shimmering, dream-like quality which is itself a judgment of the impermanence of things. Even love appears like a brush fire in her heart. Lady Ise's poems, on the other hand, are court poems. Her observation of nature is intellectual and her love poems seem written with deliberation. She is the first woman poet to reflect the highly structured ritual of the Fujiwara-dominated court.

From the time the capital moved to Kyōto, the Fujiwara family provided the royal family with wives so that the Empress and the Crown Princess were almost always Fujiwaras. Most of the men poets of the Heian Period were members of the Fujiwara clan, which eventually had to subdivide into different surnames. It was in these years that the court took on the aspects of a cult, with life as ceremoniously organized as a Buddhist ritual. To parallel the growing power of Fujiwara wives and mothers, the other court families used their daughters to gain higher rank through marriage by educating them in calligraphy, poetry, music, especially the *koto*, and in memorizing classical Chinese poetry. This produced great women writers: "The Mother of Michitsuna," Sei Shōnagon, Murasaki Shikibu, Izumi Shikibu, and Ise Tayū. They were mainly daughters of regional administrators, connected with the higher nobility by marriage and by attendance at court as ladies-in-waiting to the Empress.

No one in this list is known by her actual name. Sei, Murasaki, and Izumi are what we could call nicknames, and Shōnagon and Shikibu were either names of their husbands' offices or nicknames. The Mother of Michitsuna has no name at all. This is not due to the suppression of women to the point of non-identity, but to the fear of the power inherent in the knowledge of a person's "real" name. This is a common custom among many peoples, most of them far more primitive than the Heian Japanese.

Murasaki is the name used by the author of the *Tale of Genji,* probably the greatest novel ever written by what we could call a nameless author. Murasaki is also the name of the book's heroine. This work is in sharp contrast to that of Sei Shōnagon. Shōnagon's *Makura no Sōshi (The Pillow Book)* is a miscellaneous collection—part diary, part gossip, and part judgments on questions of aesthetics and etiquette. It is a vivid picture of a world of glamorous people and everchanging nature, lit up by a kind of noon-day beauty. It is also extremely waspish in temper, bearing a certain resemblance to Lady Wortley Montague, the friend of Pope, but without her intelligence or practical sense.

It is impossible to discuss Lady Murasaki within the limits of an essay such as this. The *Tale of Genji* is a novel of extreme complexity, unparalleled until Henry James and Marcel Proust. The greatness of the novel has obscured the beauty of the many poems scattered through it. These poems are not as randomly chosen as they might seem but are, rather, pivots in the lives of the characters and in the development of the novel. Behind the surface of the novel, and especially behind the poems, lies a profound philosophy of esoteric Shingon Buddhism of the type which would eventually become isolated as Tachikawa Shingon, that is, Left-Handed Tantric Buddhism. Recently, a leading American Japanologist has decided that it is a Shintoist novel. Most Japanese consider it a novel of protest against male promiscuity, but then few modern Japanese critics have a meaningful understanding of Heian culture. The novel's memory was blotted out by the despotic pseudo-Confucianism of the Tokugawa Epoch and the "Westernization" that followed it.

Izumi Shikibu, whose poems are collected in the anthology *Goshūi-Wakashū*, is one of the world's great love poets. She was married several times, had many lovers, and is unique in that she is the only woman poet of the Heian court who was censured in her own day for her promiscuity. Izumi was a true romantic lover, always seeking and never finding an all-consuming love. Her poems are far more sensual and directly erotic than those of Komachi. Perhaps because of this long quest for spiritual fulfillment in erotic consummation, she eventually came to write some of the most beautiful Buddhist poems of her day. While Lady Murasaki wrote objectively of a dream-like world saturated with erotic mysticism, coolly and without devastating personal involvement, it is obvious from Izumi's poems and diaries that the latter lived a life of maximum endurable personal involvement. The Western poets she resembles most are Gaspara Stampa and Louise Labé, and her poetry, like theirs, is much more convincing than the vertiginous erotic poetry of Western women of a generation or two ago. No one could be less like Edna St. Vincent Millay or Renée Vivien, who were always "on camera."

The poets representing the late Heian Period are Kenrei Mon-in Ukyō no Daibu and Princess Shikishi. Ukyō Daibu lived through the long, tragic fall and practical extermination of the Taira family. Most of her poems are written to a young Taira warrior, but it is an unfulfilled love, infinite and beyond the world.

Heian civilization was breaking up. Poetry was becoming mysteriously transparent and actual love was transcendentalized. Princess Shikishi's work was no exception. Her love strikes inward, starts, attains its extremity in secret lamentation, and floats away in the lapse of time. This is partly true because she held high social position and spent her long life as a maiden serving the Shintō gods, but it is also true because women's love became sublimated in their poetry as the feudal age closed over Japan.

In Kyoto the Emperor and his court became, as it were, priests and acolytes in an elaborate ceremonial, if powerless, rule. Government passed to the Shōguns, originally a military office—"the barbarian-fighting general." With the move of the administrative capital to Kamakura and the restructuring of Japanese society on the basis of enfiefment of warrior lords to the Shōguns, the Emperors and their courtiers ceased to have anything to do with the actual governing of the country. They ceased to control its sources of wealth, whether agriculture, mining, manufacturing, or trade.

For a little more than two hundred years the Shōgunate had its capital in Kamakura. Soon, however, the office of Shōgun itself became ceremonial and government passed into the hands of regents whose daughters married the Shōguns. The Hōjō family gained control exactly as the Fujiwara family had, by marrying their daughters into the imperial family. Society became even more rigid, what we today would call totalitarian. In retrospect, though, Kamakura seems to have had a special culture of its own, one with more connections to earlier than to later governments.

Society was dominated by the warrior caste and the so-called samurai code, *Bushidō*, a peculiar Japanese interpretation of Neo-Confucianism, became the dominant social ethic. The upper-class woman was completely subject to her husband, and her role was to bring up her children in the proper samurai spirit and to demonstrate enormous inner strength in times of crisis. The peculiar combination of promiscuity and purdah disappeared. It was inconceivable after the thirteenth century for a woman to live like Izumi Shikibu. Independent women writers were usually nuns. There was a brief renaissance of poetry in the 12th and 13th centuries under the leadership of a group of related poets beginning with Toshinari, but it slowly died out as society became more rigid. This little group of poets represented the last expression of the court poetry which had flourished for about eight hundred years. It was a group refined to the point of decadence, but it also represented an attempt to revive the great traditions of Japanese *waka*.

With the collapse of the Hōjō regents there was a brief attempt to revive the power of the Emperor, but this led to the establishment of two courts. There was an emperor in Kyōto who was ruled by Shōguns of the Ashikaga family, and an emperor in Yoshino, the mountainous peninsula southeast of Kyōto, who was descended from the rebel emperor Go-Daigo. This began a period of civil wars which eventually devastated the country and destroyed much of Kyōto, Kamakura, and many of the castle cities.

By 1500 A.D. the entire country was at war. Three ruthless military dictators in succession brought the wars to a close—Nobunaga (1534–1582), Hideyoshi, who became regent in 1584 after the assassination of Nobunaga, and Ieyasu, who became Shōgun after Hideyoshi's death in 1598. The three had brought peace to Japan, but at enormous cost. Nobunaga, for instance, surrounded Mt. Hiei, destroyed all the temples and monasteries, and killed all the monks and nuns, some 40,000, at least. Ieyasu came to power with a war of extermination against the descendants of Hideyoshi. All three of these warriors were "new" men, although they claimed connections with the old noble families. Ieyasu moved the capital to Edo, modern Tokyo, and established a Shōgunate that would last for three hundred years. These three men are regarded as the founders of modern Japan.

Through all this turmoil Japanese culture survived, but significant changes took place. Zen Buddhism became the popular cult of the military caste. *Waka*, renamed *tanka*, as the form is known today, was replaced by *haiku* of seventeen syllables. Ink painting, derived from that of the Southern Sung dynasty in China, came to surpass that of the Chinese masters, especially in the work of Sesshū. Cults of flower arrangement, tea ceremony, Noh drama, and gardening as a kind of mystical abstract art all developed during these years of turmoil. As in Europe in the Dark Ages, the monasteries preserved the continuity of the culture and at the same time gave it a new direction. *Yūgen*, "awe," the thrill of mystery and depth, became after Shunzei the dominant aesthetic criterion of Zen appreciation of art and the specially sought quality of experience itself. *Sabi*, a complex term which includes lonely, worn, long used objects, whether gardens or paintings or houses, is another special criterion. *Haiku* were supposed to capture these feelings in their finest expression.

Haiku was almost exclusively a masculine literature. Women were completely subordinate to their families and were forbidden to read the "immoral" women writers of the Heian Court. Most were kept illiterate, and if they could read at all were permitted only manuals for housewives and similar literature. In the latter half of the seventeenth century Bashō established *haiku* as an extremely subtle literary form. Directly descended from him were a few women *haiku* poets like

Chigetsu-ni and Chiyo-ni. The special caste of *geisha* took its final form in these years. Professional entertainers, courtesans, *geisha*, and prostitutes (*oiran*) learned to chant *haiku* and twenty-six syllable variants of classic *tanka* to entertain their customers. Although there were collections of *haiku* by women such as *Kiku no Michi (The Chrysanthemum Road)* and *Tamamo-shū (The Poetry of Seaweed)*, it can safely be said that during the seven hundred years of war and Tokogawa military government not a single woman writer of importance emerged. Women were oppressed under a misinterpretation of Buddhism and were taught the Confucian virtue of smothering the feminine ego.

In 1867 imperial rule was restored and Japan was opened to the rest of the world. The caste system was simplified and the freedom to choose one's residence, to marry beyond the caste boundaries, and to choose one's occupation were insured by law. Men still generally kept many mistresses, and women were discriminated against by law. Equal compulsory elementary education was established and the first women's college was founded, but conventional treatment of women prevailed and there was little freedom of speech, religion, or of assembly.

Tanka again became popular among women. Fifteen or so women novelists appeared in the 1890s and the 1900s, but it was a *tanka* poet, Yosano Akiko, who first fearlessly expressed a strong female consciousness in her *Midaregami (Tangled Hair)* in 1901. Her book was extremely controversial; some critics said that she wrote like a prostitute. In the 1890s the poets of *Shintaishi* (New Poetry) were forming the pre-Romanticist Movement centering around *Bungakkai*, the Circle of Literature. They were attracted by Tu Fu, Bashō, and Byron. Their poems, in a style imitating Western verse, had a meditative sweet sorrow.

Akiko made her start as a *tanka* poet under the influence of Heian court literature and this New Poetry of pre-Romanticism. In every way she was a prolific woman. She wrote more than 17,000 *tanka*, nearly five hundred *sistaishi* (free verse), published seventy-five books, including translations of classical literature, and had eleven children. When she met Yosano Tekkan, her future husband, he had advanced the reformed-tanka movement of his masculine "tiger-and-sword" style to inspire the youth in the days of the Sino-Japanese War, and had founded the *Shinshi-sha* (New Poetry Association) to publish the magazine "Myōjō" (Morning Star), the major literary organ of Japanese romanticism.

Compared to Yosano Akiko, the other "Myōjō" women poets, such as Yamakawa Tomiko and Chino Masako, were more traditional. Yamakawa Tomiko, who is well remembered for her three-cornered romance with Akiko and Tekkan, expresses her feelings in a strong but reserved way. Chino Masako's *tanka* were simple and clear. Akiko, Tomiko and Masako together published a collection of *tanka* called *Koigoromo (Garment of Love Making)*. Kujō Takeko, another of the "Myōjō" poets, was a writer of spiritual endurance who was preoccupied with the life of her inner self. The rest of the *tanka* poets wrote in the traditional mode, in which their lives were reflected in their descriptions of nature. Okamoto Kanoko was rather exceptional. She had some contact with the feminist movement and later became a novelist. Gotō Miyoko expressed an intense feminine consciousness in her poems on motherhood.

When we compare Baba Akiko's *tanka* with that of Kujō Takeko, for example, we understand how modern *tanka* has evolved in several decades. Surrealism was introduced to Japan in the early 1930s and came to fruition in the late 1950s and 1960s in modern poetry. Having been through such modernism, *tanka* has also overcome the realistic method. Baba Akiko's *tanka* assume supernatural images to express modern sensibility. This Akiko, a poet of brilliant talent like the other Akiko, is also active in criticism and drama.

Among the *haiku* poets in the modern age, Sugita Hisajo was by nature an erotic poet. But since *haiku* is so short a form, her eroticism could not find its full expression. She was expelled from the dominant school of *haiku*, *Hototogisu* (The Japanese Cuckoo), and later became insane and died. It was a pity that such a woman, one who truly wished to liberate herself, couldn't escape the constrictions of the traditional form of *haiku*.

Both Nakamura Teijo and Hoshino Tatsuko also belonged to *Hototogisu*, which was characterized by a world of lightness and domestic happiness. So long as *haiku* was a substitute for a sensuous diary, it never had enough power to transform reality. In contrast to these two poets, Yagi Mikajo is a writer of typical modern *haiku*, which has undergone the influence of surrealism. Of the six *haiku* poets, Mitsuhashi Takajo is probably the best. She revered Yosano Akiko and started as an orthodox *haiku* poet.

In a reevaluation of traditional culture after the Second World War, some critics strongly rejected short form literature like *tanka* and *haiku*. They insisted Japan had to expell the spirit of those older forms to establish a truly modern spirit. Having been influenced by surrealism, however, *tanka* and *haiku* have become so modern and strong in their imagery as to match contemporary free verse.

Women's liberation in Japan was first advocated by male reformers such as Fukuzawa Yukichi and Mori Arinori, who had been educated abroad in Christian ethics. In *Nihon Fujinron* (*Essays on Japanese Women*) (1885), *Onna Daigaku Hyōron* (*Criticism of the Moral Books for Women in the Tokugawa Period*) (1898), and *Shin-Onna-Daigaku* (*New Moral Book for Women*) (1898), Fukuzawa insisted on a reciprocal relationship between wives and husbands and wives and in-laws. He emphasized the importance of equal property rights and education, and denounced men for having mistresses. He thought it disgraceful in the eyes of advanced Western countries that Japanese women should have such low positions in society.

The magazine *"Jogaku Zasshi"* (Women Studies) was founded in 1885 for the purpose of elevating women. Several mission schools were set up in the latter half of the 19th Century to teach equality for women based on Christian ethics, although Confucian values of obedience were still taught in state universities. In 1890 the

"Law Concerning Meetings and Political Organization" was passed which prohibited women from joining political parties, initiating political meetings, and even listening to political speeches. The Japan Christian Women's Association and other groups immediately started Anti-Law Movements.

The first feminist movement started by publishing a literary magazine called "Seitō" (Blue Stocking, after the English expression) in 1911. The leader, Hiratsuka Raichō, gathered all the main women writers of the time and declared in the first issue that "In the beginning woman was the sun." The major goal in this period of feminism was less the acquiring of equal rights than the enabling of women to uncover their creativity. But after the third issue, until the last in 1916, they were wrestling with the social problems of women's liberation.

Yosano Akiko contributed twelve short poems, all free verse, to the first edition of the magazine. One of them is the famous poem "The Day When Mountains Move."

> The day when mountains move has
>   come.
> Though I say this, nobody believes
>   me.
> Mountains sleep only for a little while
> That once have been active in flames.
> But even if you forgot it,
> Just believe, people,
> That all the women who slept
> Now awake and move.

An anthology of modern American women poets, published recently in New York, is entitled *Mountain Moving Day*, after this poem which today is known to many feminist writers in the West.

Naturalism surfaced after Romanticism in Japan, in the years before the First World War. As Romanticism declined, Akiko became more concerned with national affairs. After traveling to Europe with her husband she began writing critical essays and actively participated in the movement for women's rights. When she wrote poems on social problems she always used free verse. Thus she stood at the intersection of *tanka* and free verse. There has been, and still is, a tradition in Japan that separates literature from politics, but Akiko dared to unite them in the struggle against the ruling class. She supported her family and the publication of the "*Myōjō*" magazine by her writings throughout her life. She is the greatest woman poet of modern Japan, and one of the great feminists in the history of Japanese women.

Magazines for women appeared one after another: "*Fujin Kōron*" in 1916, "*Josei Kaizō*" in 1922, and "*Nyonin Geijutsu*" in 1928. In the political field, *Shinfujin Kyōkai* (New Women's Association) was organized in 1919 by women such as Ichikawa Fusae and Oku Mumeo, who continued their effort to abolish "The Law Concerning Meetings and Political Organization." In 1920, women were for the first time allowed to initiate political meetings and listen to political speeches. Various groups were formed to secure voting rights for women. It is ironic that it was in 1945, when Japan was defeated in the Pacific War, that Japanese women were first given the right to vote and the right to be elected to public office.

It should be understood that modern women free-verse poets have no direct connection with main stream changes in pre-war and post-war poetry. The contemporary age can be compared to the Heian Court period in its flowering of women writers. When we look at modern women poets, however, they seem to belong more to the universal stream from the medieval period than to any movement of recent decades, though the subject matter and styles are far broader than before, having been cross-bred with Western literature and culture.

The influence of Kitazono Katsue's surrealistic modernism, through his magazine "VOU" (first published from 1935 to 1940 and revived in 1946), upon contemporary women poets is greater than is supposed. Nakamura Chio before the war, and Inoue Michiko and Shiraishi

Kazuko after the war, were the main members of this group.

Most post-war women poets belong to the so-called "social school:" Ishigaki Rin, Ibaragi Noriko, Kōra Rumiko, Takiguchi Masako, Takada Toshiko, and Fukunaka Tomoko. Perhaps the latter two should more properly be called the "popular school." Despite the long Japanese tradition of separating literature from politics, Ibaragi Noriko and Kōra Rumiko take exceptional interest in politics, the latter in a more intellectual way. Rumiko intensified her somewhat left-wing approach under the influence of Francis Ponge's approach to words and things. Ibaragi Noriko has a more direct relation to the post-war poetic movement as a member of the group *Kai* (Oar), representative of the early 1950s. Women from Osaka, like Ibaragi and Tomioka, are generally more realistic than those from Tokyo, and are tenaciously rooted in the sense of daily life. Ishigaki Rin is a typical post-war poet who writes about her place of work and her situation as an unmarried poor woman who must support sick parents. She thus discovered a fundamental way of life which Japanese women had followed for thousands of years, and although her poems seem to be anti-feminist her intention is to re-value the foundation of women's existence.

There are few feminist poets in a strict sense in Japan today. Women do not have a sense of rivalry with men, and the influence of the radical feminism that started at the end of the 1960s is just gathering strength. Individual originality is much more highly valued than a sense of feminism. Takiguchi Masako is an exception. Her prototypical poem is of a blue horse, painfully alone, dreaming in cold flames under the sea, but her poems which deal with male-female relationships are studies in women and are interesting from the viewpoint of feminism.

One feature of post-war poetry is the appearance of poems in which the speaker is not identified with the author. These are poems through which we can see a vast anti-realistic or abstract world equivalent to this world. Tomioka Taeko's poems are interesting in that she is a syntax reformer. She is the first poet in Japan who has managed to slip out of her poems, a technique she learned from Cubism and the works of Gertrude Stein, which she translated into Japanese. She gives every expression using her sense of space as a unit so her language escapes fixed significance. The reader often feels as if thrown into a state of anti-gravity. However, although her poems look very modern because of her style, they are in fact rooted in old Japanese culture and her theme is anti-modern. Her poems are presented in an ironic, sardonic way and are widely accepted in Japan as unique both by conservatives and progressives.

A typical erotic poet is Shiraishi Kazuko, who was born in Vancouver and received her baptism in modernist poetry in her teens through the "VOU" group. In her late twenties she employed an American jazz beat and adopted a counterculture life style. Until the end of the 1960s she had been avant-garde in her sexual boldness and unconventional behavior both in her poetry and her personal life, and was attacked by conventional critics. But after the revolution of sensibility at the end of the 1960s her poetry was more widely accepted.

In the latter half of the 1960s a violent poetic revolution was carried out by the poets who had come out of the turbulence of the student protest movements. They exploded the subject's energy with language, inquiring into the meaning or meaninglessness of their existence. Kanai Mieko was the youngest, and at first the only woman of this group. She unites vulgarity with holiness, Japanese songs with a French classical world view. Dream and violent eroticism is her subject both in her poetry and novels. Yoshihara Sachiko seems almost to come out of the Japanese earth, moist with karma, duty, and human feelings. In her early works she tried to re-create the genuine responses of her childhood through her own experience of motherhood. Her recent books deal frankly with the love of women, and develop a dialectic of love centered on such themes as sin, punishment, betrayal, and bloodshed. With the appearance of Tada Chimako we could for the first time say that we had a truly intellectual poet. Nurtured on European thought, from Hellenism to modern French structuralism, she has come to believe that both creation and phenomena are deceptions and poetry a false chronicle. Her poetry is concerned with the interplay of inner reality and super-reality revealed through an exploration of self that culminates in an expression of harmony that seeks to fill her absolute loneliness.

Contemporary Japanese poetry is very "Post Modern," and most of the poets are non-religious. We can, however, recognize the shadow of Buddhism in the works of some women poets, and the Buddhist influence is growing among the younger generation. The strongest influence is contemporary Western literature and culture, since translations flourish in Japan. It was the men poets who introduced the English poets of the 1930s, followed by modernism, especially surrealism, and American Beat poetry. The men have struggled to mine various veins of the Japanese language through different "movements." Women poets have been more independent. Their work seems to be marked by stronger personality and have more universality, like the great women poets of medieval and ancient Japan.

III.
Table of Japanese Historical Periods

Legendary and
Archeological

Jōmon—Ainu-like Neolithic peoples. Yayoi—infiltration and conquest by ancestors of modern Japanese. Tribal society.

100–6 00 A.D. Archaic

Korean and Chinese influence. "Empress" Jingū of Kyūshū invades Korea. Izumo and Yamato clans on Honshu.

600–710 Ancient

Imperial rule of Yamato clan, Buddhism introduced, new capital in each reign. *Kojiki* and *Nihonshoki* chronicles.

710–784 Nara

Capital at Nara. Buddhism extremely powerful. Imperial rule. Rise of Fujiwara clan. *Manyōshū*.

794–1192 Heian

Imperial rule. Fujiwara dominance. Great age of classic women writers. *Kokinshū* and succeeding anthologies.

1192–1333 Kamakura

Shōgunate, dominated by Hōjō Regents, at Kamakura. Emperor at Kyōto. Rival Emperors at Yoshino.

1336–1500 Muromachi

Ashikaga Shōguns at Kyōto.

1534–1603 Sengoku
        Adzuchi
        Momoyama

Civil Wars. Military conquest and unification by Nobunaga, Hideyoshi, Tokugawa Ieyasu. End of great court poetry. Jesuits and Dutch in Japan.

1603–1867 Edo

Capital of Tokugawa Shōguns at Edo (Tokyo). Purely ceremonial

Emperor at Kyōto. Japan closed. *Haiku*.

1867–Modern

Imperial restoration. *Haiku*. Shōgunate abolished, Japan opened, capital moved to Tokyo by Emperor Meiji. *Tanka* revival. Taishō Emperor. New *tanka*. Free verse. Shōwa Emperor. Social and "modernist" poetry. Pacific War, U.S. Occupation, Recovery, Post-Modern Japan.